IS THERE A CHRISTIAN PHILOSOPHY?

IS VOLUME

10

OF THE

Twentieth Century Encyclopedia of Catholicism

UNDER SECTION

I

KNOWLEDGE AND FAITH

IT IS ALSO THE

39TH

VOLUME IN ORDER OF PUBLICATION

THE TWENTIETH CENTURY ENCYCLOPEDIA · OF CATHOLICISM ·

Edited by HENRI DANIEL-ROPS *of the Académie Française*

IS THERE A
CHRISTIAN PHILOSOPHY?

By *MAURICE NÉDONCELLE*

Translated from the French by
ILLTYD TRETHOWAN, O.S.B.

HAWTHORN BOOKS · PUBLISHERS · *New York*

First Edition, April, 1960

NIHIL OBSTAT

Joannes M. T. Barton, S.T.D., L.S.S.
  Censor Deputatus

IMPRIMATUR

E. Morrogh Bernard
  Vicarius Generalis

Westmonasterii, die XXV JANUARII MCMLX

The Nihil Obstat and Imprimatur are a declaration that a book or pamphlet is considered to be free from doctrinal or moral error. It is not implied that those who have granted the Nihil Obstat and Imprimatur agree with the contents, opinions or statements expressed.

CONTENTS

INTRODUCTION

If a philosopher is a Christian, he has no need to be ashamed of it. But, if someone says to him, "So you have a Christian philosophy" (or, to make matters worse, a Catholic or a Protestant one), he may be hardly pleased or even extremely disconcerted. For what is really being said to him is something like this: "You are not a philosopher in the strict sense of the word, you bring in religion to bolster up your reasonings. You have certain pretensions, but have you the application and the ability which they demand?"

But it is not as simple as that; an innuendo or a witty remark is not enough to settle the matter. Jaspers wrote not long ago: "The Bible and the biblical tradition are one of the foundations of our philosophy. . . . Philosophical inquiry in the west—whether it is acknowledged or not—always uses the Bible, even when that is attacked."[1] This is manifestly true, and the problem is already before us.

No, the matter is not as simple as it may appear. Indeed a little reflection shows that it is extremely complicated. We must face the issue frankly. Is there a Christian philosophy? To a question of this sort almost any reply might be given, on the face of it, in view of very diverse conceptions which exist both of philosophy and of Christianity.

Since my intention is not to talk at random, I shall discuss several characteristic answers to our question in the hope of reaching some positive idea of what Christian philosophy is

[1] K. Jaspers, *The Way to Wisdom*, Yale Univ. Press, 1951.

and of making, if possible, a fresh contribution to the subject. So the first part of the book will deal with the teaching of the past in regard to it from the beginning of the Christian era to our own day, and the second with the famous debate which took place in France in 1931 and which set against one another the finest intellects of that country. The third part is an attempt at a profounder synthesis in which I begin to depart somewhat from the usual conventions of language: it is to be considered as a mere rough sketch—there is not room for further development within the limits of this volume.

It is important to note that it is the *notion* of Christian philosophy with which I am concerned, considered both historically and in itself. It is not my intention to draw up a *programme* for a Christian philosophy or to fill in its *content* by writing the various chapters of a treatise (the existence of God, the immortality of the soul, the function and purpose of matter, etc.). These are the subjects of other books in this series, particularly those which immediately follow this and which analyse the masterpieces of our traditional religious philosophy from a less limited point of view.

AUTHOR'S NOTE TO THE ENGLISH TRANSLATION

The plan of this book has obliged me to compress much information and much discussion within the compass of a few pages. After reading through the original text, written in 1956, I feel tempted to add fresh chapters and many notes. But by doing so I should exceed my allotted space. I must at least remind my readers that my historical interpretations need justification which, to my regret, I cannot properly supply.

The last section, in which I offer my own attempt at a solution of the problem, also calls for supplementation. The subject is a difficult and controversial one, and of this I am keenly conscious. What I have to offer is not a definite thesis but a working hypothesis. My purpose has been not to conclude the debate, but to stimulate it and to warn people not to be content with theories based on insufficient evidence. Where need arises, I have taken certain liberties with language, and I hope that my purpose in doing so will be borne in mind.

I also ask the reader not to isolate particular reflections from their general context, and this seems to me particularly important in two instances. The examination of conscience which I urge upon "critical" philosophers (pp. 120–2) is a rather painful one. But in showing that we shall not get far in philosophy if we confine ourselves to logistics, I have been very far from decrying the reasonableness of a complex criteriology which I employ myself throughout the book and which is at the furthest possible remove from mere uncontrolled feeling. The immense success of logical positivism in the English-speaking countries, and the timorous fideism of some religious philosophers which has been its consequence, are among the strangest and most distressing phenomena of our time.[2]

Secondly, I have suggested the use of the expression "supernatural metaphysics". It is no bolder than "Christian philosophy", although it sounds more provocative. Three problems are to be distinguished here. To what extent and in what respects is there a metaphysic which finds in Christianity

[2] I have made my protest against these tendencies in an article on "The defeatism of the new British Theologians" in *Revue des sciences religieuses* (1957), XXXI, pp. 169–80.

itself: 1. its source; 2. its constitutive activity; 3. its formal object? It has seemed to me that if one allowed the influence of grace at one of these points, one could not fail to allow it at the other two also—but to a certain extent and in certain respects; this last restriction must not be forgotten. What Suarez maintains about the *lex connaturalis gratiae* might be applied here: and there are also useful suggestions in the work of Vittoria, for whom the divine wisdom has set its mark both on the order of grace and on that of nature.

To put everything into a nutshell, I would say, in the first place, that a Christian metaphysic is possible because metaphysics cannot evade the problem of integration, and in particular that of human integration, on which Blondel and his school have rightly insisted. Then the possibility of such a metaphysic follows from another consideration which is no less important and which is bound up not so much with an interior summons as with the verdict of history. In this world persons are the source of ideas and principles which translate a personal existence into an organism of notions and thus help to reveal the fundamental nature of things and the virtualities of the human reason. Now the person of Christ is the source of ideas and principles which can give a supernatural quality to metaphysics. This is the case when a philosopher comes across and incorporates into his synthesis certain views about Providence and the Incarnation or certain new values which have become visible among men since the life of Jesus upon earth. These elements can become philosophical if they are considered in abstraction from the person from whom in fact they derive and are examined in their effects upon creatures rather than in the life of God himself to which they refer us; unlike the materials of theology, they are thus detached from sacred history and give rise to processes of thought which are not in the immediate orbit of theological faith or in direct relation with an event in the revealed order.

They can, therefore, enter the sphere of ontological inquiry and enrich it analogically, although they are not cut off from the gifts of an infused wisdom and are destined, no doubt, in the total perspective of salvation, to prepare the way for an acceptance which goes beyond the powers of pure philosophy.

PART I

THE TEACHING OF THE PAST

CHAPTER I

PHILOSOPHY IN THE EARLY YEARS OF CHRISTIANITY

What did the word "philosopher" mean in the time of Christ? A man, Plato had written (*Republic*, 475 b), who "loves wisdom in all its forms", that is, someone who devotes the best part of his life and his best energies to the search for truth, to discovering the first principles of things and to setting his life in accord with them. Cicero says plainly enough: "We call philosophy all knowledge of the highest things and all conduct in accordance with it." It is the synthesis of all the greatest acquisitions of the human mind and it influences conduct. Definitions of this kind were collected in handbooks and circulated among educated people. Since they were vague and indicated a tendency of mind rather than a definite doctrine, they were accepted by everybody and were a part of the inheritance of Graeco-Roman civilization. So much can be said at least of certain maxims common to all schools of thought which had for long expressed the idea of Greek wisdom, such as the celebrated Delphic oracles, *nothing in excess, know yourself*, or the advice given by Solon to Croesus and repeated in one of La Fontaine's fables: "In all things, one must keep in mind the end."

But during the centuries there had been very many philosophers of very different kinds around the Mediterranean basin, and if we are to move beyond banal generalities and form a concrete idea of what philosophy meant we must consider the various schools. First we may consider the dogmatists. Some of them were above all eager for knowledge; they were theorists, proud of their learning and convinced that they could get to the bottom of everything and see all round it. Their tendency was to be encyclopaedic, at any rate the Platonists and Aristotelians among them. But the thinkers who were most in the public eye put the emphasis on morality or the art of living, and pure theory was not much in favour. People were looking for a recipe for happiness and peace of mind. This was supplied by the Epicureans, although their doctrine was not a particularly cheerful one. For them the world's progress was a very limited affair. No doubt the original disorder of the atoms provided opportunities for evolution, but the general structure of the universe was soon formed; the meeting of the elements produced solid masses and the impetus of vital forces very soon died down. The only way which is still open is that of the individual's moral progress, for it is always possible to attain to the serenity and even the enjoyment of life which Epicurus recommended to his disciples. Unfortunately, most men are fools, and do not know how to secure a happy life by restraining their desires. The Epicurean aims at happiness alone or with a few friends and is quite unconcerned about everybody else.

The teaching of the Stoics was similar to this extent that for them also the fundamental problem was that of tranquillity. Their answer to it was the avoidance of the passions, "apathy". But the human reason as they conceived of it was far more enterprising. For example, the inquiring spirit of Posidonius (135–51 B.C.) was impressive: he was of eastern origin, like many Stoics, being born at Apamea in Syria, and had incorporated Platonism and the sciences of his day into his system. The philosophical activity of such masters had an engaging quality about it, they had a very keen sense of human solidarity, and they believed that the physical universe was ruled by providential laws, and that reason penetrated everything, so that each reality was a sort of mirror of the whole; but their practical opposition to all forms of disorder made them champions of asceticism and caused them to put the emphasis on moral values. They formed the most flourishing school of thought at the beginning of the Christian era.

Alongside the dogmatists, whether theorists or moralists, was a second group of philosophers, the sceptics. Their sharp-witted rationalism made them excellent destructive critics. They were always seeking and never finding, true to their name (σκέψις means inquiry). They cast doubt on everything, even on sensation, so far as this involves a judgement of the mind. They set out the arguments on either side and took the line that there is always another side to any argument. So wisdom lies in suspending judgement and deciding nothing in the affairs of the intellect. The sceptics philosophize in order to destroy philosophy. In the ordinary affairs of life they are far from being revolutionaries, as one might have expected, but rather for the most part attached to traditional ways. Why change things? What do I know about it? Just because I cannot decide anything with certainty, it is simplest to live as custom decrees. So the sceptics are often supporters of the established religion. Nevertheless—and this is a point to which we shall return—they sowed a seed which produced an unexpected harvest. An irrational fideism lies in wait for a philosophy which can bring no certain answer to life's problems.

The third group of thinkers which offered itself to the inquiring minds of the time was that of the mystics. This was not the title by which they were known as a rule, for it belonged properly to the mystery religions and we are speaking of something very different, of philosophical speculation. But we may call all these people mystics for the sake of convenience and because they have a certain affinity with religion. More and more, in fact, the philosopher of the Hellenistic world appears as a saviour of mankind and has the air of a propagandist. He claims or transmits a revelation, he bases his reflections on the idea of another life, he prepares his hearers to receive messages from on high; at the least he tries to relieve anxiety about man's destiny. Travelling preachers appear and certain regular convictions are found present beneath the variety of their teachings: there is a supreme divinity who is adored by all men under different names and who must be approached by the way of humble service. This God delegates his powers or his attributes to intermediaries, the heavenly bodies, which are thought of as living gods. On the eve of our era, astrology was carrying all before it; the worship of the stars was finding its way into every system. This is the moment at which the whole world is persuaded (the epistles of St Paul allude to the fact on several occasions) that there are seven heavens and that after death one must rise through them to approach God and so to complete the soul's pilgrimage. The great thing is to find well-disposed guides for one's journey and to prepare oneself for it in this life.

Philosophers of this sort tended to put themselves under the patronage of Pythagoras, or Orpheus or some legendary hero; these were still called mathematicians or theologians, but categories became rather confused on the fringes of these corporations. They were, to repeat, religious propagandists of a profound, sometimes rather pathetic, kind rather than reasoners in search of objective truths. What was the reason for the burgeoning of these multitudinous sects which are so hard to distinguish and to classify but which are akin to one another in their latent monotheism, their mediators and their pilgrimages beyond the grave? Fr Festugière insists on a very early cause which takes us back to Plato himself. Plato had been horrified by the atheism which he saw growing up all around him. In his last dialogues, in the *Laws* and in *Epinomis* (which he inspired if he did not draw up), he wanted to rescue young people from the corrupting influence of the sophists. To this end he elaborated a theology which recognized an ineffable God beyond all essences and, a little lower down in the scale, a cosmic God. The latter, who is better able to attract the prayers of the multitude, must be honoured in those stars which have autonomous movement; he must be the object of an official worship, protected by the State and sanctioned by the Law. In the most classical Greek literature, then, we find a tendency to a very special form of monotheism, accompanied by astrological beliefs which will become fashionable several centuries later.[1]

Next one should show what Hellenistic speculation owed to Alexander the Great. According to Plutarch, Alexander said that God is the common father of all men. The statement is perhaps apocryphal, but we know that in 324 the conqueror summoned Macedonians and Persians to a common banquet and solemnly took to wife a daughter of Darius. His clear intention was to establish a universal empire and to break down the ideological barriers between the different countries. In the enlarged and precarious world which he left behind him, exchanges had become easier and more frequent; divinities harmonized instead of conflicting and Zeus ὕψιστος could pass for an analogue of the God of the Jews.

In the troubled centuries which followed, a feeling of general breakdown passed quickly from the sphere of politics

---

[1] A. J. Festugière, *Personal Religion among the Greeks* (Berkeley, Univ. of California Press, 1954), chap. III.

into that of speculation. The individual became aware of himself, thanks to the collapse of local institutions; he acquired the sense of his personal liberty but through a menace which threatened him on all sides; he felt himself abandoned in an absurd world and handed over to chance. Fortune became the supreme principle and certain cities minted money in honour of this goddess. E. R. Dodds considers that the horror experienced in face of this sort of liberty led to the introduction of exotic doctrines. To escape their obsessions men were forced to take up with consoling day-dreams. In Rome and in Greece also fantastic beliefs were elaborated under the influence of Babylonia or Egypt.[2] They added their prestige and success to the traditions which Plato had interpreted in his old age. The civilized world had a growing taste for these wares from abroad and especially for those from the East. Epicurus alone warned his disciples of the dangers involved in astral theology: all the other schools succumbed to the "Chaldaean" spell. Among the Stoics in particular there was a sort of "treachery of the learned": Diogenes of Seleucia, one of the leaders of the Stoa, is an example of this in the second century before Christ, although Panetius, his pupil, tried to check the movement.

Such, in very rough outline, is the picture presented by the tendencies which were becoming more and more marked during the Hellenistic period. What is to happen when they encounter Christianity? Religious desires and an interest in revelation seem to promise it a favourable welcome. Many partial and implicit agreements seem inevitable. Furthermore every event has its atmosphere, and if the coming of Christ was the new event the pagan philosophies were one of the elements in the atmosphere. The first group which we have distinguished, that of the dogmatists, had made a great effort,

[2] E. R. Dodds, *The Greeks and the Irrational* (Berkeley, Univ. of California Press, 1951), chap. VIII.

almost an excessive one, to be accommodating. They were ready to look beyond the limits of their systems, despite their most inveterate slogans. The thinkers of this group had in general the sense of contemplation and a certain piety. They did their best, if not in Europe at least in Alexandria, to consider one another as brothers in spirit. They would have Plato and Aristotle brought together and the two parties allied in an ecumenical philosophy.

The Stoics often took the lead in this movement towards unity. And if we take Stoicism as the most characteristic example, we can find easily enough Stoic dogmas which are in harmony with Christianity or prepare the way for its message or facilitate its diffusion. Stoicism professed faith in a Providence, whose wisdom disposes all things so well that we are never at the mercy of chance; it professed faith in a Logos or Word which unites us to God. The source of all reason and the maker of all things, which comes down into us and penetrates us, fortifies us and brings us back to heaven. Intimately present in each man, the Logos was at the same time the binding principle of all humanity; we are of the same race as he, and through him we make contact with the basic energies of this world and the hidden things of the next. But the Stoics were not always pantheists; the absorption in God which they professed has been the subject of a good deal of exaggeration. One of these founders, Cleanthus, left behind him a hymn to Zeus in which he begged God to open the eyes of sinners and to convert them, a passage of unprecedented significance which has been too little noticed. Posidonius, also before the opening of the Christian era, is said to have erected an altar to his "daemon" or ideal self at which he offered worship, a sign of a keen awareness of personality and of personal vocation. Seneca's esteem for the reason went with an equal esteem for the self: we are a part of God, he said, but he added at once that we are cooperators

with him—in a theory of man as a microcosm the two statements are perfectly compatible and do not imply pantheism
in the usual sense of the word. Epictetus in the same way
extols his personal dignity in a way which is commonly
thought to show great pride but which does not prevent him
from calling himself the servant and the psalmist of God.
In point of fact it was not the Stoics who recommended the
west and the world at large to merge all minds into one another and into God. On the contrary, they attributed a moral
grandeur to God; some of them seem to have taught the
notion of creation and made known to us, before the time
of Christianity, the eminent value of the human person.
According to them, we are radically superior to the brutes:
furthermore, it is for us that Providence has created everything else, a bold claim which would have shocked Plato and
exasperated Plotinus, but which seems pretty evident to most
Christians.

Like the Christians, the Stoics turned their faces against
exclusiveness and parochialism because they professed a limitless philanthropy. Their outlook was cosmopolitan, and they
regarded the social distinction between masters and slaves
as of minor importance. But they had a keen sense of the
moral maladies which afflict and weigh down the generality
of mankind. They even asked themselves whether there was
a single sage among them who was really a complete man,
really exempt from every folly. Their pessimistic view of
things was something new; they made much of mental patho-
logy, in opposition to the more soothing conception of nature
entertained by the Greek thinkers. What efforts were needed
to bring the elect to wisdom! Philosophy in their hands
becomes a work of salvation. It is practised like a religion to
rescue sinners from evil ways, not by collective measures but
by an ascetic vigilance over one's own conduct and with the
aid of a director. This led them to evolve a casuistry and, in

particular, a psychotherapy. The Greeks had often compared philosophy to medicine and maintained that it was the art of healing souls: Epictetus gave this commonplace a quite special emphasis. And Seneca declared: "You have been summoned to aid the wretched; they beg your help, and their lives are in danger." The true wretchedness, in a sense the only one, is spiritual failure. So the cure of souls, their conversion, is the sage's preoccupation. Jews and Christians could not agree more.

Finally Stoicism had an eschatology. It proclaimed that the world would come to an end; it put before its adepts the thought of a universal conflagration. All the realities with which we are familiar are to be gathered together into their principle, which is living reason, in a moment of tragic consummation. The history of the universe consists in periods of successive expansion and contraction. For all we know we may be at the end of a period of expansion and our dying world may be hastening to the final catastrophe. This theme too fitted in easily enough with the apocalyptic mentality of the Semites which so strongly marked the early Christians. It is true that the Stoics believed in an eternal rebirth while the Semites had a linear conception of time, but beneath these different appearances the intellectual sensibilities on either side were parallel or even convergent.

If we find among the dogmatists elements of thought which contributed to the rapid formation of a Christian philosophy, we find even more in other schools. Let us leave aside the sceptics with the reminder that they were bent on paradox and could give no answer to the demands which men were making. Their effect on the better spirits of the time was in large measure, and despite themselves, to bring grist to the mystics' mill. And of these last there is much that might be said. They were eager for revelations and ready for spiritual adventures. They had no desire to acquire a state of tranquillity or to exalt "apathy"; they were on the look-out for novelties even if these were disconcerting for the traditions of their countries or disturbing for the mental equilibrium. Philosophy in their hands is not so much an affair of the discursive intelligence as of inner experience, imagination, feeling, intuition, even ecstasy. This sort of emotional outburst in which so many uncontrolled images are deployed cannot be a safe ally for Christianity; yet it can blaze a trail, for Christianity after all was not based upon learning or upon technical discussions as a means of finding the truth, but on purity of heart, obedience to God the Saviour, the proclamation of good news from above.

To come down to particulars, let us first note that the pagan mystics insisted upon the divine transcendence. The Most High is worthy to receive prayer, honour and service. But it is quite impossible to attain to him without those intermediaries who emanate from him and who raise us to him. Next, these doctrines were dualist: they did not attenuate the reality of sin and suffering, nor did they overlook the desire for relief, for purification and salvation. Lastly, they had a demonology: they gave warning against the danger from evil spirits who rove about the world, and they outdid them, sometimes by magical formulas, sometimes by subtle reflections and sometimes by efforts of moral sanctification. Certainly Christianity had other axioms and a different atmosphere, but connections between the two mentalities were easy to find. Philosophers were better placed for observing this in that they took over into their systems, and transposed in the process, the cruder aspirations of the common people which were exploited by the diviners and soothsayers. In hermetic circles, as in the mystery religions, the flame of a very pure and personal religion sometimes burnt brightly.

In fine, the pagan autumn had tints enough to match each Christian belief or attitude. Men's capacities for accepting the Gospel were now fully developed. Suppose, for example, that an educated person had read the recommendations in the sixth chapter of St Mark's Gospel: "And he [Jesus] gave them instructions to take a staff for their journey, and nothing more; no wallet, no bread, no money for their purses: to be shod with sandals, and not to wear a second coat. You are to lodge, he told them, in the house you first enter, until you leave the place. And wherever they give you no welcome and no hearing, shake the dust from your feet in witness against them." Such words would have been strangely reminiscent of what the Cynico-Stoics recommended to their disciples. These people, rather like mendicant monks, who have been called the Stoics of the hovels, could understand better than others the avengelical counsels which have just been quoted or again the meaning of the beatitudes and the precept of turning the left cheek when someone has struck you on the right. For them the sage had to be an ascetic (halfway, according to a classical distinction of antiquity, between the disciple who has to learn everything from another and the autodidact who no longer needs a master). Our educated person would certainly not have understood that the Christian ascetic was moved by the love of Christ, but he would have acknowledged that wisdom ought to make him patient and even that he should sacrifice himself for another. Gladiatorial shows are said to have been abolished by the heroic devotion of two Cynics and a Christian, St Telemachus: that was, however, in a century when Christianity had had plenty of time to affect the current philosophies.

It may perhaps be objected that these affinities do not touch the real problem. Yes or no, had pagan philosophy the wherewithal to adapt or to adopt the most fundamental beliefs of the new religion? The question demands a careful answer. The Graeco-Roman sage did not lack sympathy and openmindedness, but he was limited by his own presuppositions. He could bring to the consideration of revealed truth a set of categories which should, by their nature, have smoothed the path for him, but in embracing Revelation he often stifled it. What seemed most propitious for a meeting between the two mentalities was at the same time the means, could he have successfully employed it, of abolishing his new ally altogether. A whole network of ideas encouraged him to give Christianity a welcome. But what a danger this was for Christianity itself! Take, for example, the Christian belief in the Trinity. Just as there were sects who could praise the poverty, humility and love of the Gospel, there were others who were disposed to admit into the world of the divine a plurality which did not conflict with the purity of the supreme principle. The unknown and ineffable God who is beyond all things had mysteriously and eternally given birth to a cosmic God who was his incarnation: he was in a sense inferior, but how close he was to his Father and how high above ourselves! Later, in the second century after Christ, Numenius and Albinus distinguished three levels in the divinity: highest of all is the God who is beyond all essence, then the God who is a thought which thinks itself and whose ideas are the "demons" (powers) or "reasons" on the model of which everything else has been brought into being: finally, on the third level, God is the astral mover who controls our earth. Thus there is a sort of multiplicity in God, although unity is safeguarded at the topmost point. This is not the Christian Trinity, but at a certain distance and *grosso modo* it could be mistaken for it, especially before the Council of Nicaea. Armed with such a system a pagan could suppose that he was grasping the thought of Christians; he was offering them an articulation of their ideas which they were at present lacking, and in doing them this service he provided them with an excellent means of going astray, as the Arian heresy made very clear.

Or, again, take the Incarnation itself. The idea of a God

who comes down among us out of sheer generosity is not altogether unknown in pre-Christian times, despite some statements to the contrary. In Philo, whose work is so important for understanding how Greek and Semitic ideas came together, the Logos is diffused among men, unites them together and brings them back to God, their common Father. Eusebius could even take Philo for one of St Peter's disciples. Can we go further and allow that the pagans sometimes conceived of an *individual* incarnation of the divine principle? If we are to believe M. Carcopino, the notion was in the air.[3] Thus the Stoic Cornutus, almost contemporary with Christ, assimilated to the Logos the God Hermes, who is charged with conducting human souls to this earth and bringing them back again to heaven. Hermes of Cyllene is a highly individualized figure, with the golden rod with which, according to Cornutus' commentary on the Odyssey, he touches the eyes of men to enchant them. The writers of this period see universal symbols in particular events and explain mythology by the apotheosis of human beings. Cornutus also considers that "Heracles is the Logos diffused through all things, who gives nature its strength and power".[4] The allegorizing philosophers had no need to feel disconcerted by the claims of Christianity; they could exclaim, as Hindus do today when they listen to a Christian missionary, "Why should not God be incarnate in Christ? He has been incarnate already in so many!"

Furthermore paganism had a *gnosis*, a dualist explanation of the existence of evil which, if accepted, would hasten its reabsorption into good. This pious doctrine implied a fall, human or divine, the preexistence of souls, a condemnation

[3] J. Carcopino, *Le Mystère d'un symbole chrétien* (Paris, 1955), p. 58.
[4] Quoted by M. Simon, *Hercule et le Christianisme* (Paris, 1955), p. 95.

of matter, the intervention of demonic powers, and a gospel of salvation. *Gnosis* was a hybrid affair, grandiose in its ambitions, cloudy in its developments, and it was the instrument by means of which paganism might have dissolved Christianity into eastern mysticisms. It had one of its centres at Alexandria, another in Palestine. A single name may sum up the snares and hazards to which such a movement exposed the early Church: that of Simon Magus. Living at the crossroads of Samaria, the meeting-place of so many cults and ideologies, Simon immersed himself in Old Testament, Persian and Hellenistic traditions at the same time. He built up the first Christian philosophy, and the result was a spectacular set-back. But who could deny the fascination of this sort of thing for his contemporaries?

According to Gnosticism, man is to be described as an inferior form of wisdom, emanating from God, which has been defiled by its separation from him: it is brought back by God or by an emissary of God. Here again the idea of a Providence which is moved by man's wretchedness is incontestable. God sends his Son to look for the lost sheep, as Simon himself said, drawing on the Old Testament and post-exilic Jewish literature. A theory on "the celestial man" was added to this scheme of redemption—perhaps it came from Jewish writings about Adam. If one considers that gnosticism was held in honour among the Essenes with whom the community of Qumran was connected, one begins to get some idea of the intellectual and spiritual turmoil which accompanied the first manifestations of Christianity and which must have made its originality hard to discern at first with any clarity.

The background against which the religion of Jesus developed was therefore highly complex. Post-exilic Judaism had accepted and digested more than one Persian or Greek notion. Sometimes indeed it digested them badly, and heterodox groups were formed as a result. Conversely,

Judaism was infiltrating more and more into pagan wisdom. So far as the latter was concerned, the New Testament might have been taken over as well as the Old, witness, for example, the *Codex Jung* recently discovered in Egypt or the *Shepherd* of the hermetical writings which shows such a familiarity with the Pentateuch. The Christians had before them not only possible allies but also thinkers who presented them with distorted reflections of their own minds. Fortunately they had from the first a very lively sense of their originality, and took upon themselves once and for all the task of proclaiming and safeguarding it.

CHAPTER II

THE NOTION OF CHRISTIAN PHILOSOPHY UP TO ST AUGUSTINE

At first Christians were not at all eager to construct a Christian philosophy. They were suspicious of the compromises and the pitfalls which such an enterprise would have inevitably involved. They realized that they were not as other men, and they dug themselves in. In any case their competence was not one of the intellectual order and they did not fancy themselves as professors. The New Testament refers to philosophy on only one occasion and then in order to warn the faithful against its dangers: "Take care not to let anyone cheat you with his philosophizings, with empty phantasies drawn from human tradition, from worldly principles; they were never Christ's teaching" (Col. 2. 8). The passage shows the radical difference which St Paul makes between his doctrine and others: on the one side, there is a wisdom founded on the fashionable astrology (that is the meaning of "worldly principles" here; on the other, the foundation is Jesus, a historical personage, unique and irreplaceable, he who reveals God and saves all men by his life, his word, his death and his resurrection.

St Paul, of course, has no hesitation about using philosophical ideas in certain circumstances; in his speech on the

Areopagus, he speaks of the unknown God and quotes from Cleanthus or Aratus: "We are his children since it is in him that we live and move and have our being." He also avails himself of the Stoic commonplaces about man's knowledge of God: "From the foundations of the world men have caught sight of his invisible nature, his eternal power and his divineness, as they are known through his creatures" (Rom. 1. 20). That is why men are without excuse when they are ungrateful or negligent in his regard. One has the impression that St Paul recognizes the existence of a power of reason immanent in all men which dictates to them the elementary rules of conduct. He refers casually to certain norms of commonsense; for instance, he considers that the State should ensure good order by attacking injustices and restraining criminals. By the same token he can recommend his correspondents to follow all that is good and just and holy. But philosophy in itself has no interest for him, and he has no use for the wisdom of this world, which seems to him quite empty and incapable of fulfilling its promises. He knows that he has a very different message to deliver. This message, like that of the New Testament in its entirety, is that God loves us, staggering news which blazes out with a joyful intensity in which the pale benevolence of a philosophical divinity has no part. Nothing in the ancient world and nothing since in the modern world have rivalled these accents. It is astonishing that historians should have tried to get round this fact and to make comparisons. The Christian God is without comparison. He bursts upon human awareness as a complete novelty, unless we can compare a few pipings scattered over the preceding centuries with this overwhelming symphony which suddenly resounded for men to hear in all ages. God loves us; and so we can love him, and so we should love one another. The staggering news has been expressed in a man in whom dwelt all the fullness of the divinity: a crucified man who has come out of his tomb alive and of whom Paul can say: "For me, to live is

Christ". This was a revolutionary statement if ever there was one, senseless for the Greek philosophy of ideas and scandalous for Jewish or Gnostic piety. A personal relationship has been established between Christians and the presence of Jesus: his life, which animates the Church, nourishes the most intimate recesses of their personalities. He inserts us into himself only to make us free and to make us our true selves, a strange sort of causality which is not among the categories of the sages and which by the power of its presence is something much greater than the bond which bound a legendary Hermes to his clients, greater even than the intimacy of Adam with Yahweh his Creator. Henceforth God is with us, God is in us, for he has shown himself to us in Jesus who has lived among us. A concrete existence and not a system of ideas or entities, that is what manifests, inexhaustibly and for all time, God's reality.

St John's attitude, when he comments on the life and death of Christ in the Prologue of his Gospel, is in no way different. He speaks of course of the Logos, and people have supposed that he borrowed it from Hellenism. In fact he did borrow something non-essential, just enough to show that we cannot relate the Christian Revelation to the mentality of the Jewish people alone. The Logos has a long history in Greece: in Heraclitus it is a material fire which presides over change; in the Platonists it is the intelligible world, the home of Ideas: in Stoicism it has astonishing complications—it is the organizing force of nature, it is the thought and speech of man, it is the reason conceived of as identical with God, and it is the master, the mediator and the original world-stuff all at the same time, although it refers especially to the world-soul; in Gnosticism, on the other hand, it is a message from on high, an "aeon", the revealer who emerges from the silence in which the ultimate principle of the divinity lies hidden. But the Logos has also a Semitic basis: the last books of the Old Testament and apocryphal Jewish literature more or less personify the creative Word, Wisdom, the Name of Yahweh or the revealed Law, ideas which are sometimes very close to the Greek Logos. The *Wisdom of Solomon* identifies Wisdom with the Word, God's only daughter. In Philo the Alexandrian Jew, born about 20 B.C., the Greek and Semitic traditions unite in such a way that the former is at the service of the latter. At the first stage, the Logos is an uncreated attribute of God, always in act; at the second, it is the system of the ideas and is thus a creature of God anterior to the physical world. In the third and fourth stages, it is the Word which is immanent in creation and which in some sort intercedes for it. Philo calls it, according to the various aspects of it which he wishes to indicate, the first-born son of God, older than all creation, the second God, the incorruptible image of God, and even the ideal man. God creates the world by him, so as to give us a model to imitate—not because God needs an intermediary but because in his goodness he wants to help us and to bring the extremes into harmony. All this is so striking that Fr Lagrange has not hesitated to write an article on Philo entitled "Towards the Logos of St John".

Yet St John's originality is complete. Not only does he associate with the Logos of the Greeks the Jewish theme of Yahweh's glory, thus making it transcendent, but he also radically transforms the Logos of his predecessors. He has given to a term which was not Philo's property, and also had in all probability only a vague meaning to the generality, a quite precise sense. He has made of it a real person and not a personification, whereas even in Philo one can still sometimes ask oneself what really emerges, an abstract principle or a concrete conscious being. Again, St John clearly attributes the divine nature to the Logos, without any of the vacillations or complicated connections with the world which we find in Philo. Lastly, he carries out his most thoroughgoing rehandling of the materials by a series of definite distinctions and designations: the Logos is identified with the Jewish Messias;

the latter, in conformity with devout expectations, is identified in his turn with a Saviour who sacrifices himself for men; and the Messias is localized in the historic person of Jesus, who introduces the last times. It is this last claim which would have scandalized a pagan or a convinced Jew. To the question asked by Gentiles and the children of Israel alike, John gives an unexpected and ridiculous answer: the Logos is Jesus who was crucified under Pontius Pilate. This being whom he declared to be the creator and the light which enlightens every man coming into this world is also the being whom the disciples approached, with whom they lived on familiar terms and of whom they now give witness. He it is who reveals God to us because he is God, and so his Incarnation must be complete and unique. Although the Fourth Gospel is full of signs, this shows conclusively that there is no trace of allegorism in the manner of Cornutus, who could extend his Logos sometimes into Hermes and sometimes into Heracles, without bothering much about the person who lent his name to the divine substance; Cornutus was perhaps moving towards concrete expression, but certainly he never formulated the idea of an irreplaceable individual.

To make possible a notion of Christian philosophy from which Christians would not shrink in horror as from a piece of trickery, a dialectic in three stages was therefore necessary. First there was a preparation of the Gentiles for the Gospel, parallel with that of the Jews and sometimes taken over by them: this preparation could direct attention to the new religion, but it could not simply unite with it or adapt itself exactly to it for, by the nature of the case, it would not provide the sudden novelty of a living and personal individual. So the second necessary stage was the shock of experience, the manifestation in time and space of this unpredictable being, Jesus, although his life on earth established only some of his characteristics, as a face is only partly revealed by a picture. In the third stage the principles and ideas which had heralded the coming of Jesus had to be brought together in his person; there had to be a refashioning of all that had been previously achieved, which without him would have remained a collection of dispersed elements or arbitrary syntheses, since there would have been no true centre on which they could converge.

Christian philosophy could come to birth only as a result of the impact of Christ and of reflection upon that impact. We are very far from the subtle process of hellenization of which Harnack spoke, as though the historical Christ had been progressively eliminated from the minds of Christians in proportion as they fell back into philosophizing. We are very far also from the contamination of the message of love (*agape*) by a supposedly egoistic desire (*eros*) as Nygren maintains, as though the Gospel of St John had already substituted for the disinterested grace of God a too human eagerness for perfection and as though later theology went on to replace a divine generosity which comes down to man and sweeps him into its own movement by a pagan philosophy which tries to make itself the proprietor of the greatest of all goods and to evacuate the mystery. What actually happened was something very different. There was, and so long as there are Christians there always will be, an initial datum, which is the dazzling light of Jesus, and then a remodelling of everything else under his influence: the latter is just as necessary as the former, and is in no way a betrayal or denial of it.

A casual glance at things certainly suggests that the historical Christ has been overlaid with the sediments which profane culture and worldly considerations pile up on the devotion of the faithful or on theology. The danger of travestying what one reflects upon is not chimerical. But faith cannot last if it does not live, and it cannot live unless it acts upon the cultures or the instincts with which it comes in touch. The risk of infidelity to which it is exposed is much greater if it remains inert than if it tries to extract with its existing resources the meaning and the consequences of a past event. The chimera, in this case, is the ideal of pure perception; and the wisdom which the Gospel itself demands is only to be gained by a progressive reflection which penetrates the tradition so as to obtain all its fruits and to transform our whole being by contact with it. It does not much matter if our ideas seem to go beyond the Christian message or to replace it by something else. What matters is not the lump, but the leaven. What matters is faith in a person who gives a meaning to ideas and engenders them.

In the place of a salvation gained through the knowledge of philosophy the Christian puts salvation gained through the redemptive action of a person. That is why the concept of Christian philosophy took time to make its appearance and to free itself from possible misunderstandings. We do not find mention of it, in the documents which remain to us, until the second half of the second century. Even so it is hardly developed. Tatian lays claim to Christian faith which is, he says truculently, "our barbarous philosophy" (ἡ καθ'ἡμᾶς βάρβαρος φιλοσοφία). He was repeating what had been said, although without defying the Greeks, by his master St Justin, the first Christian whom we know to have claimed the title of philosopher and to have declared that Christianity is a philosophy, "the only sure and profitable one". In his *Dialogue with Trypho*, Justin compares his conversion to a philosophical pilgrimage. After following masters of all sorts without finding satisfaction, he met a wise old man from whom he gained the secret of the truth. He was a Christian. Justin learnt from him at last that the truth is a fact which is handed on by testimony and not an explanation resulting from the mere initiative of the seeker. The true philosophy is in the word of the prophets: "They did not speak in demonstrations. Above and beyond demonstrations they were the worthy witnesses of the truth, but it is past and present events which make one accept what they said." The philosophical problem presents itself to us and receives the beginnings of an answer, but the complete solution comes from the Scriptures and from Christ. Why then does St Justin set such store by the title of philosopher? First of all it is because he claims to present a rigorous argument and to demonstrate what he believes, but also because he perceived explicit affinities, which he frankly acknowledges, between the witness of Christians and the statements of Plato and the Stoics. But why is there this affinity? There is nothing surprising about it. And here St Justin takes up an idea from Philo: the Jews have been robbed by the Gentiles; Plato is the heir, consciously or unconsciously, of Moses, and the riches of the Greeks are the spoils taken from the prophets. This way of writing history makes us smile; the claim is altogether excessive, but it is not entirely without foundation,[1] and we have ceased to believe in the miracle of an isolated Greece which gave to the east and received nothing in return.

The similarity between the two wisdoms is also to be accounted for, according to Justin, by a deeper reason. The Word who has manifested himself fully in the historical Jesus has always acted upon men's minds in an invisible way, and apart from the machinations of the devil he would have done so much more. He makes his truth available to every race and time. He enlightens thinkers who pass for atheists in the eyes of their contemporaries, such as Heraclitus or Socrates among the Greeks. The Word, in short, is the reason in which the human species participates, and those who live in accordance with this reason are Christians, even if they (or we) do not know it. This generous apologetic marks the conscious and systematic adoption of Platonism into the speculation of the Fathers.

The consequence is obvious: all that is true and good in the history of thought is at once the property of Christians. They

[1] The tradition according to which Plato went "to the prophets in Egypt" (Diogenes Laertius, III. 6) goes back to Hermodorus of Syracuse, the master's immediate disciple. See F. Daumas, *Bulletin de l'Association G. Budé* (March, 1956), p. 113.

must recognize and promote within the fold the fragmentary visions which the Gentiles received outside it. This is an ambitious theory, but it proceeds, to repeat, from a generous faith. Humanism has been restored to the Church. Is the thought which inspired Socrates or Heraclitus the divine Word itself? Is it an image of it, a "seed implanted", an initiation? The difference matters little for our purposes. What is certain in any case is that participation in the divine wisdom has been foreseen by Providence on a very generous scale. The historical character of Jesus is no obstacle to the truth of philosophy, because it both brings it to perfection and is prepared for by it. The Word has been made flesh not in order to contradict Plato but to share our sufferings and to bring us a remedy for them, that is, to be with us in a sense which Plato could not imagine.

After Justin nothing new along these lines is to be expected. The essential has been already achieved. We find, however, many anti-liberal writers, who are so jealous for the treasure of God's kingdom that they turn upon the philosophers in anger. Tertullian, for example, some fifty years after Justin, is unwearying in his sarcasms on the subject. For him heretics and philosophers are all one; they ask the same questions, explore the same field, puzzle over the origins of evil, the purpose and destiny of mankind, the constitution of the universe and so forth. They produce their answers in terms of obscure principles which they suppose to be apodeictic but which are really pedantic or absurd verbalisms such as ἐνθύμησις (conception) or ἔκτρωμα (abortion). "A curse on Aristotle!", Tertullian exclaimed, "Down with Stoic, Platonist or dialectic Christianity! Since the coming of Christ, we have no more need of subtle theories or investigations, for we have the truth and we should be foolish indeed to entrust ourselves to shifting sands." *Credo quia absurdum* is attributed to Tertullian. Is it a piece of pious irrationalism? Not necessarily. Tertullian knows well enough that God is the

Father of lights, but he believes that the divine light dazzles our eyes with its splendour and that our minds, coarsened by sin, are too dull to understand the thought of heaven. This hostile attitude to philosophy is to some extent shared by the great St Irenaeus, an admirer of Plato but much concerned with extirpating the gnostic heresies. It will always find its defenders among the Fathers, either because they are incapable of philosophizing or because they consider that dogma cannot enter without damage into a system from which mystery is excluded. But Justin's attitude becomes more and more the dominant one.

Clement of Alexandria holds that philosophy is a gift from heaven which prepared the Greeks for the Gospel rather as the Law educated the Jews. Its pedagogic function was not only beneficent but necessary. The Alexandrian Fathers, strong in the faith which overcomes the world, made offers of peace and alliance to the civilization with which they were surrounded. The situation has completely changed since the time of the initial conflict with philosophy. Then the powerful pagans seemed ready to approach Christianity with a sympathy which was dangerous for it, and the Christian minority, scenting the danger, held itself aloof. But by the beginning of the third century Christians had nothing to fear from misunderstandings; they offered their weakening adversaries like Celsus and Porphyry, who were putting up a desperate resistance, a scheme of Christian philosophy which implies the liquidation of paganism in the name of the Logos himself.

Origen fills out this scheme with an extremely rich content; his speculations about freedom delight by their own freedom, and his breadth and fertility of mind remain unequalled until the Middle Ages. But we are concerned here only with his method, which is that of Justin and Clement with a *nuance* of its own. This great man sees in everything reflections of the One Necessary Being; his tendency is to give to the supreme *gnosis* a sort of exaggeration, to the detriment of what we should call today "temporal values". The created world exists only to be passed by. Origen always seeks for the divine model behind finite beings; he becomes air-borne at once, and does no climbing. Sometimes one could wish that he would come down more to earth. Faith guides him in all his inquiries, yet he is not simply a theologian; if he does not graft faith onto a philosophy, he does graft a philosophy onto faith; the parent trunk is Christian, but the branches are of diverse kinds and concern only a chosen few among the more educated of the faithful. So in the *Peri Archon* Origen examines at his own risks and perils a number of problems for which faith provides no definite answer: the origin and the incorporeality of the soul, the nature of the angels, the dialectic of liberty, the plurality of successive worlds, the animation of the stars. . . . Even when he speaks of the Trinity he finds a place for disputed questions which go beyond the deductions which are required by faith although they remain within the field which it throws open to us. This free speculation, which does not leave the legitimate domain of a meditation on the faith but which operates in it without claiming the general assent of Christians, seems to be what Christian philosophy becomes in Origen, although the distinction was not explicitly made by him and had yet to receive expression. The frontiers are certainly far from clear; Origen's allegorism, which is in fact a spiritual realism, leads him to look for a sign of God in every visible event or element, and nowadays we should assign such interpretations either to religious philosophy, or to theology or to edifying literature as the case might be.

St Augustine presents his readers with fewer enigmas, and his influence is far greater; he dominates the Middle Ages, representing and summing up patristic thought for that period. He often said that true philosophy is one with true religion and true theology. These different expressions are synonymous in his vocabulary, as opposed to the religion, philosophy and theology of the pagans, and the expression "Christian philosophy" occurs for the first time in his work. The wisdom of the ancients was not, in his view, superior to that of the Christians, for theirs alone is perfect. Unlike the thought of classical Greece, it essentially involves the invocation of a living God, as in the Hellenistic epoch. But it is perfect because it depends upon the only revelation which is not illusory, that of Holy Scripture. If philosophy is the love of wisdom, absolute wisdom is God himself; since God is known to us by faith and faith finds the revelation of God in Scripture, the philosophy of Scripture is the true philosophy. This line of thought, as Prof. Gilson very rightly remarks, enables us to grasp the precise meaning of the famous aphorism *credo ut intelligam*, I believe in order to (or, in such a way as to) understand. Philosophy is not shut off from the believer's deepest convictions; it inevitably translates them. It is true that the opposite formula *intelligo ut credam*, I understand in order to (or, in such a way as to) believe, also has its truth: the previous use of the reason leads us towards the Word and disposes us to recognize it by faith. But the second maxim is not fully clear except in the light of the first. *Credo ut intelligam, vera philosophia est vera religio*, that contains the Saint's original and fundamental thought.

At other times he insists on the fact that philosophy is not everything and practically jettisons its equivalence with true religion. In the *Confessions* he remarks that he has read many truths in the Platonists. "But that he came to his own and his own did not receive him . . . that I have not read in these books. . . . That the Word was made flesh and dwelt among us, that I have not read." Sometimes his reservations receive still greater emphasis: philosophers easily become presumptuous, at any rate those who are not also Christians, like the sages of ancient Greece or unbelievers of the fifth century who have not yet laid down their arms before Christianity. They have said true things about the Father and about the

Son (that is, about the Word), but they have not known the concrete humility of the Incarnate Word, and they have said nothing about the Holy Spirit; the Godhead remained partly hidden from them. A passage in the Seventh Book of the *Confessions* sets this judgement in a serene light: philosophers are like messengers standing on the top of a hill; they see the true home-country in the distance, but they cannot pick up the road which leads to it. It is not their function to reach the goal; in spite of their prophetic gift they fall short of it, and this is what distinguishes them from Christians. They move as best they can in the direction of Revelation, but they move by their own efforts and that is why they can neither discover it nor put anything in its place.

However, the very inclination to search comes to them from grace, and the theory which we have just sketched is thus still in accordance with St Justin: it is the same idea of a Logos which is incomplete among the Gentiles and complete in Christ. Augustine always professed it and he declares in *De Doctrina Christiana*: "As for the theses which are true and compatible with our faith sometimes enunciated by those who are called philosophers, especially by the Platonists, not only must we not suspect or shun them but we must take them over for our own use as one takes back one's own goods from an unlawful possessor. . . . This precious gold which they have from God and which they offer to false divinities we must take back from them and consecrate to the service of the true God." Following this line of thought the Augustinians refused to admit an isolated, separate philosophy, but they distinguished several stages or levels of reflection. Faith is the summit to which everything leads and from which everything proceeds anew.

Thus there is now a definite divorce between the *gnosis* of the heretics and the Christian philosophy inspired by the Platonism of the Fathers. The Gnostics grant philosophy the privilege of exploring all the secrets of God and explaining them without residue. The Christians are brought to a halt before a mystery which demands the mind's submission. In philosophy, we participate in a creative and enlightening Word: in faith, we adhere to an incarnate and redemptive Word who surpasses our reason. Even Pseudo-Dionysius, in whom extremes meet, has to introduce an obverse and a reverse into his synthesis; he distinguishes "a theology which is hidden, mystical and symbolic which unites us with God, and another which is manifest, better known, philosophical and demonstrative" (Epist. IX, quoted in the article "Théologie" in *Dict. de Théolog. Cathol.*, Col. 344). However Christian philosophy wants to be or is, it cannot follow faith without becoming short-winded. John Scotus Erigena, in the ninth century, tries to deny it (*veram esse philosophiam veram religionem convertimque veram religionem esse veram philosophiam*), but his agnosticism, inherited from Pseudo-Dionysius, puts everything back into the melting-pot, because the "divine names" do not give us God himself. We need some word other than "philosophy" to designate reflection which is concerned directly with Revelation; and that is "theology." This word too had a long history, since it had been employed by Greek thinkers even before the time of Socrates, and it receives its new meaning in the Church's vocabulary at the hands of Abelard. The dividing line between supernatural theology and philosophy was drawn at last.

The principle of this distinction is virtually present in St Justin and St Augustine: Plato is a landmark on the road which leads to Jesus and not the equivalent of Jesus. But for them, and *a fortiori* for Origen, a man must be Christian in all his thinking: philosophy cannot be itself if it is cut off from the faith, and so it is Christian in this sense; otherwise it could only be a state of error and in danger of apostasy. Such is the balance-sheet of early Church history in our field; such is the challenge which these first centuries threw down for the thinkers of the Middle Ages and of our times.

CHAPTER III

HOW SCHOLASTICISM GRADUALLY LOST THE NOTION OF A CHRISTIAN PHILOSOPHY

The Carolingian Renaissance was chiefly an affair of grammarians, that is, of literary culture. Speculation was not in vogue. John Scotus Erigena who lived, it seems, between 800 and 870 is a splendid exception, and his bold system of thought is a solitary firework display. The incursion of the Normans into England and their ravaging of France, in addition to the general insecurity of the ninth century, resulted in the ruin of the monasteries and the breakdown of intellectual life. In 910 William of Aquitaine founded the monastery of Cluny, and in the following year Rollo was baptized: then there is an awakening. It must be added that interest is now concentrated much more upon the rhetoric and dialectic, the latter being organized round the logical treatises of Aristotle, Porphyry and Boethius. In time it gave rise inevitably to philosophical inquiries which gradually freed themselves from its yoke. Theology, of course, presided over all these studies.

How did philosophy obtain its autonomy in Christendom?

That immediately raises the question of the relations between the theologians and the dialecticians. Berengarius of Tours, in the eleventh century, opted frankly for dialectic, for reason seemed to him unquestionably the best guide in the search for truth. A characteristic statement of his is often quoted: "It is the mark of a great soul always to have recourse to dialectic, for that is to have recourse to reason, and not to do so is to repudiate man's greatest glory, for it is reason that is the image of God in him." So, leaving aside sacred authorities, he adopted it as an axiom that if everything is to be understood everything must be criticized. Unfortunately he applied this principle to the Eucharist. Without denying the real presence he claimed to explain the mode of it, and he did this in such a way as to deny the transformation of the bread and wine into the body and blood of the Lord—hence a series of condemnations disturbed his long life. But it would be a mistake to think of him as a rationalist philosopher indifferent or hostile to the faith; rather he was a theologian who chose to use reasoning rather than the texts of the Fathers for the elucidation of dogma. He required logical coherence in a system of beliefs instead of a synthesis formed by a mosaic of quotations. His ideas were not well received by his colleagues, and the result was a crusade against all dialecticians.

The theologians, on the whole, were so conservative that they regarded the liberal arts as useless and dangerous. Peter Damian, the Bishop of Ravenna, compared dialectic to a humble attendant upon religion, and the formula caught on. That is the origin of the phrase *philosophia ancilla theologiæ*. But did he leave philosophy even this rôle? He compares it to the devil more often than to a servant. Even grammar seemed dangerous to him, for it accustoms one to all sorts of fictions and licences, such as putting the word "God" into the plural. Peter Damian's conception of religion was that of a rigid code literally interpreted. His indifference to the rights of reason led him to adopt the remarkable thesis that if God had judged it right he could, in his omnipotence, have abolished a contingent past event. It is true that the holy man reached this conclusion on the basis of an ethically respectable voluntarism and was far from making God a capricious tyrant. His thesis originated in a typically medieval debate: "Could God restore virginity to somebody who had lost it?" The reply which is offered to us begins by pointing out that we do not know the ways of God, but our author later becomes more adventurous. If, he says, some poor girl has been surprised and violated against her will, God could blot out of existence this deplorable incident. A historical truth, in this case, can be taken out of history. God can do no evil, but he can bring about a contradiction provided that it is a morally good one. Extremes meet: Peter Damian, in his campaign against dialectic, employs the extravagances of dialectic. He reached practically the same result as Anselm of Besate, who, by elaborating a remark of Aristotle's, found a half-way house between two contradictory propositions. Such opponents combined to deny the possibility of a Christian philosophy, for they abolished the very basis of all philosophy.

The monk Lanfranc, a more moderate person, sought for a middle course. He admitted and welcomed dialectic as a way of expounding dogma. He had some affinity with the mystics, but he was above all a man of action and wrote nothing on ambitious lines. His more emancipated disciple, St Anselm of Canterbury, was, on the other hand, one of the most original thinkers of the century. Born at Aosta in 1033, he ruled the Abbey of Bec in Normandy before becoming an Archbishop in England. He died in 1109, after suffering more than one exile: this gave him some opportunity for writing and cannot therefore be regarded as altogether unfortunate. We owe to him a famous and controversial proof of God's existence known as the Ontological Argument (the conception of a being greater than which no being can be conceived implies the existence of such a being). He also worked out a theory of the Redemption based on the satisfaction which only the Man-God can offer God in justice. To these two titles to fame a third may be added which may perhaps surprise some readers and which I shall try to justify: for the historian of philosophy, Anselm is the first of the scholastics to indicate in any definite way the existence of an autonomous philosophy, that is, one which is independent of theology.[1]

At this point we must guard against misunderstandings. It would be a misunderstanding to suppose that we are dealing here with a rationalist who owes no obedience to religious authority, on the ground that he takes "necessary reasons" as his guide. If Berengarius remained an Augustinian, so, *a fortiori*, did St Anselm: he believes in order to understand. In his most abstract treatises he often mingles prayer with his reflections, and his text is studied with devout invocations which imitate the *Confessions* of St Augustine. His philosophical work is, in fact, the meditation of a believer, and the *Proslogion* bears the sub-title *fides quaerens intellectum*. Moreover he is addressing believers: his readers are monks, and he is giving them, fundamentally, what they were used to, that is to say, *lectio divina* or a commentary on the Scriptures. Although in the *Monologion* he debates with himself, and although in the *Proslogion* he is speaking to God, he is in reality writing for Christians. It is for them, first and foremost, that he takes up his pen.

This being so, how can philosophy be autonomous as he conceives it? There are several reasons which perhaps have not been sufficiently noticed. Let us take first the *Monologion*. In the first chapter we read that if a man is ignorant of God's existence or of certain divine attributes and if "this ignorance

---

[1] I shall make a certain distinction later, in Part III, between autonomy and independence, but I consider them here, provisionally, as synonymous.

results from his *lack of instruction* or his *unwillingness to believe* he can, by his own powers, even if he is of only ordinary intelligence, prove [these truths] to himself, at least in great part, through the use of reason alone". The words which I have italicized force me to qualify what I was saying just now: St Anselm is certainly addressing Christians, but they are Christians whose minds may be attacked by sloth or by doubt; he does not exclude the unbeliever—he considers him as a possible reader. And he goes on to put himself in the unbeliever's place, to produce in his own mind an imaginary unbeliever so as to let him reason or to reason with him. By virtue of a reasoning process we may move from ignorance or denial to an affirmation of God. This attitude contains in germ a philosophy which remains Christian because it is fecundated by the faith, but which becomes autonomous because it is comprehensible to a mind detached from the faith and because it confines itself to a method which is purely dialectical.

The *Proslogion* is still more instructive in this respect. Here the "fool" (who says in his heart "There is no God") is indispensable for the development of the Ontological Argument. This imaginary personage is brought on the scene at once and sets everything in motion; he is the opponent who by his denial makes the proof effective against himself. The believer who addresses other believers in this discourse is also engaging in discussion all the time with an unbeliever. The latter denies that the unsurpassable is inevitable and possessed of existence; and in so doing he contradicts himself. Nevertheless, in spite of the "fool", the *Proslogion* can be taken in one of two ways: it can be presented to believers from within the faith or to unbelievers from outside it. The confessional character of the work is immediately neutralized: it does not belong simply to spirituality or to theology, but, on at least one side of it, to a rational discipline which acknowledges only its own norms and its own exigencies. This is the discipline which will bear witness that the unsurpassable, the divine, is inevitable and that God really exists; it will even go on to show that he is pure being.

This conclusion is confirmed by another passage from the *Proslogion* which also has been somewhat neglected by commentators. At the end of chapter four we read: "I give thanks to you, good Master, for what I have first believed through your gift I now understand through your light so that, *even if I were unwilling to believe in your existence, I should be unable not to realize that you do exist*" (*etiam si non crederem, non possem non intelligere*). The illumination of the intelligence is a gift of the Holy Spirit which rewards reflective faith; that is the theologian's way of putting it, and he is quite right. But the philosopher and the historian, looking at things from the outside and on their own level, may observe equally well that this gift is a lasting gain for our nature. This is a considerable addition to the text of St Augustine quoted at the end of my first chapter: "If I did not believe, I should not understand" (*nisi credidero, non intelligam*). Everything seems to suggest that the intelligence, once galvanized by faith, retains the effect even after the departure, real or supposed, of faith. Even if the philosopher ceased to be a Christian, the image of God could still survive in his intellect as a residual consequence of his previous faith. Faith thus plays a liberating rôle: it releases and intensifies the lower power of intellect. This is a thesis which is a sort of anticipation of Franciscan thought: it would have delighted St Bonaventure. It helps us to understand *how* Revelation influences the intelligence and gives it its own independence. St Anselm, no doubt, is thinking not of the group but of the individual. But one may see in his doctrine something like a prophecy of what has happened in the civilization of the west, when the rise of deism in the eighteenth century proves to be inconceivable apart from the Christian centuries which preceded it. From the point of view of the religious philosopher the Enlightenment retains certain positive elements, for it is the heir to a grace which it overlooked or misconstrued.

If we forget this rather depressing illustration, St Anselm's suggestion, taken with the other elements which we have discerned in his thought, presents itself to us as an attractive novelty. It amounts to saying that philosophy can be Christian in its origin and in its final purpose on the one hand, and autonomous in its method on the other. If we bear in mind that its scope is limitless, since the *Monologion* and the *Proslogion* boldly pursue their chains of reasoning into the mystery of the Trinity, while the *Cur deus Homo?* shows the necessity of a redemptive Incarnation to undo the work of sin, it must be allowed that this construction is on a scale which is almost alarming, which makes one's brain whirl. For St Anselm theology is inside the movement of thought; philosophy is the outward and visible aspect of this movement which, in principle, everybody can follow, understand and accept. The change from one to the other comes from a change of perspective and of interlocutor. As each of us can put himself in thought outside of himself and in another's place, the theologian can engender a philosophy, if he wishes, within his own consciousness. And this philosophy can remain even when faith departs, which shows in a new way both the primacy of faith and the independence which the necessary conclusions of reason have acquired: they are inevitably posterior to faith, but they have their own consistency, and their structure, once formed, stands on its own basis.

It is of little importance that St Anselm sometimes refers to "suasions" rather than to really necessary conclusions. He never claimed that the philosopher's task could reach an end; always, on the contrary, he maintained that the human reason operates in a sphere which goes beyond our powers of understanding. "We see where the stream flows from", he declares, "but we do not really grasp the source from which it rises."

All the same he wants to find chains of solid reasoning, and not only probabilities, so far as this is possible. He uses dialectic, no doubt, not to explain and deduce the divine prerogatives, but to distinguish them by a sound method. In this sense his ideal is to understand everything, he knows that he will never attain to it completely, but it provides him with a very neat solution to the problem of combining a theology which is faithful to the exigences of grace and a philosophy which is fully aware of the capacities of the human reason.

Such a conception is far more complex than the view of St Augustine. He had admitted that one must seek to understand before believing: he knew by experience that philosophy can prepare the way for conversion to Christianity instead of obstructing it. Later, meditating on faith, he had recognized that in good logic it presupposed rational activity. But when the soul discovers the humility of the Word Incarnate it has no more need of the philosophers, for it has passed beyond their stammerings. From now on the task of the intelligence is no longer to lead a man to Christianity but to apply itself to Christianity and to take Revelation as the principle of its reflection. Philosophy, then, had been only an antechamber. With St Anselm, on the other hand, it gains more lasting and more glorious titles, for Christianity requires or produces a philosophical attitude which is needed at least for use outside the fold. The philosophy of the believer is the art of releasing in the believer the belief which is hidden within him, making use of the data and the reasoning power which the unbeliever finds within himself. But it would be poor-spirited to allow such a demonstration nothing but an apologetic rôle. Called in to defend believers against the attacks of atheists or to persuade the atheist that he is inconsistent with himself, philosophy is quite obviously more than an apologetic: it is an awareness of a community between the human mind and the divine mind, and it is a joyful search for moral and intellectual truth according to criteria whose force we immediately appreciate.

But this attitude, too, was to undergo far-reaching modifications in the twelfth century. Honorius of Autun, who defends the rights of reason in demonstration with some asperity, inquires whether God created men for their own sakes or to fill the places left vacant in paradise by the fallen angels. Following St Augustine, St Anselm had not hesitated to adopt the second point of view: man is not the centre of the universe, but only a sort of second-best angel, which amounts to saying that he has no great importance in himself, is not an end in himself. Honorius, on the other hand, considers that if all the angels had remained faithful to God Adam and all his posterity would have been created just the same. He thought the other view absurd. Let us concentrate on the visible world and the beauty of its organization, he seems to say to us, and leave day-dreams alone.[2]

This down-to-earth humanism was much encouraged by the discovery of Aristotle. In St Anselm's time Aristotle was known only to some extent, chiefly as a logician and through the eyes of neo-Platonic commentators. About the middle of the twelfth century translations of his works on physics and on ethics began to appear, and a century later he was still all the rage. At the request of St Thomas Aquinas, William of Moerbeke revised previous translations of Aristotle and undertook new ones. As the Greek text of Aristotle became better known, so also his Arabian disciples were studied, and it is chiefly owing to them that the peripatetic philosophy was so highly valued. Now in Islam Hellenism had flourished quite

[2] It is true that Honorius could invoke the authority of Genesis and claim that he is only bringing out the logic of the Biblical story. However, Anselm's opinion seemed at first sight to safeguard more effectively the glory of God and the disinterested love which should be given him. So St Thomas tries to reconcile the two theses.

otherwise than in the Christian countries. The Aristotle of Arabian scholasticism was materially more complete than our own, but by no means less adulterated. There had crystallized around his name all the astrologies and some forms of *gnosis* which had been current in the ancient world. The doctrine of the active intellect, which had been re-fashioned in the first instance by neo-Platonic writers, had been adapted by the Arabians to a theology in which God was everything and man almost nothing. The physical universe was conceived of as a cycle of events controlled by the hierarchy of the stars in a rigorously determined pattern. The new astronomers substituted for Ptolemy's epicycles a system of homocentric spheres which moved from east to west under the action of a single mover. In this vast and simple setting everything had its place —except the Gospel. Thus a neo-pagan philosophy had come into existence, shunned by some Christians and welcomed enthusiastically by others. At the heart of Latin Christianity there were to be found admirers of Averroes like Siger of Brabant, who was led by philosophy to conclusions which were opposed to Revelation and thus found himself in a very uncomfortable position, since he continued to adhere personally to Christian truth. Even St Bonaventure could not reject Aristotle root and branch. But for the thorough-going Aristotelians natural wisdom was sufficient for all purposes, and the respect accorded to Revelation was hypocritical. Thus St Bonaventure complains of the approval given to this sort of system, and in 1270 thirteen propositions of the extremists were condemned by ecclesiastical authority. They were the following: 1. there is only a single intellect; 2. it is incorrect to say that man understands; 3. the human will desires or chooses of necessity; 4. everything is subjected to the necessity of the heavenly bodies; 5. the world is eternal; 6. there was no first man; 7. the soul corrupts along with the body; 8. after death the soul cannot undergo corporeal fire; 9. the power of choice is passive and is moved by desirable objects; 10. God has no knowledge of individual beings; 11. God knows nothing outside himself; 12. human beings are not guided by Providence; 13. God cannot give immortality. No author was mentioned by name, but the errors thus listed had been taken either from Aristotle or from Parisian doctors. The latter were more particularly envisaged in a fresh catalogue of 219 errors stigmatized by the Bishop of Paris, Stephen Tempier, on March 7th, 1277.

That was the third anniversary of St Thomas's death, and he was among those condemned. Had he, then, also abandoned Christian philosophy and denied a creating Providence, human freedom and the soul's immortality? He was soon to be exculpated. But he had wished to baptize Aristotle, and this alone shows us how far we have travelled from St Anselm. Just as the Gothic Cathedrals show us a style very different from the Romanesque, so Thomism represents a mentality, even perhaps a civilization, very different from that of tenth-or eleventh-century Augustinianism. The difference is not due simply to the introduction of Aristotle; it shows a whole new outlook, a new way of regarding the relations between faith and reason.

The human reason, in fact, claims independence. For St Anselm it does so in the perspective of an initial supernaturalism; for St Thomas it has its own parallel establishment, inferior to Revelation, but originally and in principle independent. For in the understanding of nature, in discussing the meaning of an ancient text—in a word, in philosophizing—authority is the weakest of all arguments, even the authority of faith. For testimony is one thing and critical examination (which everyone can conduct, Christian or non-Christian, in virtue of his natural powers of judgement) quite another thing. The *Summa contra Gentiles* even undertakes to defend Christian dogmas one by one against the infidels, adopting their own rational point of view. This is a philosophical apologetic, not a theology. In this respect the position of

Duns Scotus will be the same: one must not "abuse nature".

"Few theologians", remarks Fr Chenu of St Thomas, "have pushed so far what we should call the discretion of the faith and the principle (which is the source of this discretion) of the scientific autonomy of reason in its own domain." Thus he takes great care to avoid all supernatural considerations when he is discussing problems in the natural order. The mockery of unbelievers seems to him justified when an argument confuses the two spheres and becomes an incoherent pious amalgam. The title and the content of St Thomas's short work *De aeternitate mundi contra murmurantes* are significant in this connection; he maintains that one cannot rationally prove the absurdity of a world which had no beginning. So much the worse for those who grumble about it! The information which Revelation gives us must not be smuggled in to rescue the philosopher in his difficulties or to supplement an argument which relies only on natural evidences. Under those conditions, the idea of a Christian philosophy is at bottom hardly conceivable: it sounds as shocking as a Catholic geometry. We must allow that, with the coming of Thomism, the notion which we saw developing in the patristic period is, at least in appearance, broken down. Either we know something or else we believe it: when knowledge supervenes, belief has no longer a place. Philosophy and Christianity can no more mix, if I may so put it, than oil and vinegar.

The most striking thing of all about this new synthesis is its air of calm confidence. The anxiety, which sometimes becomes anguish, of St Augustine has disappeared. Thought now moves in an ordered course, coolly, without visible emotion. There lie the greatness and the limitations of St Thomas; he conducts his analysis as the imperturbable spectator of being and beings. Furthermore the ground-plans of nature and of grace seem to him given once for all: the world's plasticity is not of any importance. When the natural order is under consideration, St Thomas has no difficulty in accepting Aristotle's wisdom with its aristocratic bent: he brings the soul nearer to the body, he almost entirely subjects the individual to the species, he does not worry about slaves, and natural beatitude is bounded by a very terrestrial horizon. The Christian in him certainly turns these proportions and these propositions upside down, but as a philosopher he is positive, one might almost say positivistic and extroverted, if such labels could be applied to so great and so generous a thinker.

For it must be allowed that his naturalistic tendency is made supple and subtle by insight of great penetration. He considers the human individual in the cold light of reason as a part of the community, but at the same time he tells us that the active intellect belongs to individuals and that intellectual substances are governed for their own sakes, not for others; in an admirable passage he explains that the intention of nature is directed to what is permanent: thus by reason of his soul the human individual is nature's chief consideration and therefore escapes from the complicated system of things which are mere means to ends. So long before he reaches the supernatural order in which each human being is an image of God, he has corrected the paganism of his premisses.

Nevertheless the hierarchical universe which he describes contains some surprises, perhaps some scandals, for a Franciscan soul: even when we allow for the effects of the feudal system, it is strange to learn that slavery is natural in view of the good which results from this institution on the whole (and this good is that of the masters); we are still with Aristotle or Seneca. It is no less strange to read the passages about the purchase of baptized slaves, in which the distinction between the natural and supernatural levels of being is taken over into the juridical field. If the slave of a Jew becomes a Christian, he must be put on sale within three months and the baptized *vernaculus* will be freed without monetary compensation. "In this the Church commits no injustice, for, since the Jews themselves are the servants of the Church, she can dispose of their goods" (IIa–IIae, Qu. 10, art. 10, resp.). Side by side with passages such as these are others in abundance of the greatest value for a Christian spiritual personalism, and it would be going too far to claim that they have yet been synthetized or that their implications have been fully worked out.

The notion of a Christian philosophy, we were saying, seems to have been abandoned by St Thomas. Such a conclusion would need a great deal of qualification. Thomism infuses into a vocabulary of Greek and Arabian origin new ideas about God, the creation of the world, and the destiny of man, and although these ideas are justified by the use of reason they have been formed in St Thomas's mind by his Christianity. Moreover in the hierarchy of the sciences, philosophy is crowned by theology just as nature is by grace. One and the same God works and is reflected on both levels of being; the one Truth lavishes its variety over both levels of speculation. In fine, St Thomas, like most men of his time, is much more interested in the supernatural life than in nature. He fixes his eyes on the coping-stone, not on the pillars or the buttresses of the building; his philosophy never has the first place in his thought. The revelation of divine truths in the natural order (such as the existence of God and his attributes) is morally indispensable for sinful humanity; if reason were left without assistance, these truths would be known only by a few choice spirits and, even so, not without the admixture of many errors. In short, the Thomist philosophy is Christian, if by that one means that it came to birth in an atmosphere of Christian reflection, that it leads normally to Christ, and that, despite its internal autonomy, it must give way to the requirements of faith if there should seem to be a conflict between the two.

We may go still further. In the light of the intelligence, where the intellect resides together with the first principles of philosophy, God summons and guides us. He does so, not by dividing himself up or substituting himself for our own judgement, but by bringing it into activity. The consequences of this mysterious influx are such that Prof. Gilson finds here at the heart of Thomism a certain debt to St Augustine. It is fundamentally the divine light of our intellects which justifies the possibility of Christian philosophy. On this showing, various interpretations of Thomism which sharply separate philosophy from grace, and are treated as axiomatic by the manuals, are doubtless in need of revision and begin to look like misunderstandings.

After St Thomas the balance was not preserved: people went to extremes. The fourteenth century, as M. de Gandillac put it, is the "century of clean breaks".[3] This is not true of the Franciscan John Duns Scotus, who was born in 1266 and died prematurely in 1308. Despite his criticisms of Thomism, he was no extremist. He takes account of Aristotle and Avicenna as well as the Augustinian tradition of his order. God is for him the unsurpassable and the infinite discovered by a rigorous meditation on being. Did he reduce the number of attributes which, according to St Thomas, philosophy can discover in the infinite being? This is a debatable point. The primacy which he gives to the individual and to the will does not hamper his tendency to multiply essences and thus to encourage speculation in the study of God and of the world. Whether one likes his approach or not, it is neither more nor less Christian than St. Thomas's although it is Christian in a different way.

The Averroists, on the other hand, could give rise to legitimate alarm in the Church. Their most brilliant centre was now at Padua, but even in Paris, in 1324, John of Janduno and Marsiglio of Padua in their *Defensor Pacis* exalted the

[3] Fliche and Martin: *Histoire de l'Église*, XIII, p. 332.

totalitarian state and subjected the Church to it. They constantly evinced their contempt for the theologians: their true guide is a human reason which concentrates upon events and individuals; it provides them with certainties which often prove contrary to the faith, and although in an extremity they yield to faith the homage which they pay to it is unconvincing. Averroes had taught that the truth which is in itself accessible to the wise appears only in a symbolic form in theology and in a popular form in the Koran. The Latin Averroists, more crudely, invented the theory of a "double truth": reason and faith contradict one another.

The reaction against them among the fourteenth-century scholastics succeeded in making any Christian philosophy even more impossible. In this connection William of Ockham (1290–1349) is the most important figure. He was a Franciscan, but his thought is directed against Duns Scotus, especially in his ban upon the search for essences in the name of a principle of economy ("entities must not be multiplied without necessity"). Metaphysics has overweening ambitions: its wings must be clipped. It can prove the existence of God only with great difficulty: the series of causes cannot, indeed, go back for ever, but is there only a single first cause? Reason can arrive only at probabilities in this matter. The beings of this world are individuals. Ockham does not believe in the objectivity of general ideas; he is a "nominalist". Relentlessly he demolishes all the abstractions which his predecessors considered to be real, including relations. From this holocaust emerges only the extremely vigorous and subtle logic with which our friar furbishes his redoubtable armoury. He claims to be on the side of faith and is fighting for evangelical purity. And he is bold enough to do this by attacking the papacy not only in the name of poverty but in that of the Emperor. He inaugurates the *via moderna*, a new way of thinking, of feeling and even of praying. Clearly he is one of the precursors of the Reformation. Working along his own lines, Nicolaus of Autrecourt goes still further since he becomes a complete sceptic in regard to Aristotle and advocates a practical Christianity to replace the shattered philosophy of the Schools.

During this period the Dominican Eckhart (1260–1329) was pouring out mystical discourses of rare power in the German-speaking countries: he had the originality to preach a doctrine of union with God by means of the intelligence, not only by love. Religion and philosophy are all one in this experience, and they are not distinguished from the Christian's inner life. The generation of the Word and the creation of the world are brought dangerously close together, and the devout soul is so much absorbed in God that sin and time seem to disappear. His distinction between God and the deity has been much attacked on the ground that the latter is set above the former. Nevertheless Eckhart does not deliver us over to abstractions, but adores a living and transcendent God. When he seems to be confusing the soul with God, he is giving the word *"is"* the sense of *"make be"*: the copula (the link betwen subject and attribute in a proposition) does not here express an identity or a logical implication or a mathematical equation but God's creative action. At the fine point of the spiritual intellect which gives him his perspective he was more orthodox than he appeared. Perhaps he was trying to express in philosophical terms the doctrine of the Mystical Body, as Mme Ancelet-Hustache maintains, or that of the Trinity, as R. Otto suggests. He certainly exercised a profound influence on his disciples, such as Tauler and Suso, whom nobody can consider heretical. His mystical doctrine is altogether an interior affair; he has no interest in "rapts" and seeks for God in all things with complete freedom of spirit, without attaching importance to sacraments or institutions. His mistake was to put too much philosophy into his Christianity, but still more to make his notion of philosophy too Christian.

Medieval scholasticism disintegrates and collapses in the scholasticism which succeeds it. Only the school of Ockham continues to flourish, and in changing forms which do not concern our subject. We have only to note that the idea of Christian philosophy no longer exists in the sense given to it by St Anselm or St Bonaventure or even in the less obvious Thomist form. We find nothing but groups of extravagant thinkers, some believers only in worldly experience and logic, others anathematizing the knowledge of this world and taking refuge in an extreme fideism, others again like the chancellor Gerson (1363–1429) trying in vain to conciliate their contemporaries and concentrating upon a "persuasive theology" which is attractive from the point of view of Christian humanism but too vague and insipid for the lover of ideas. Apart from this last school, the final period of the Middle Ages rejects all Christian philosophy because it explicitly rejects any common measure between the thought of God and that of men. Nature operates on the one side, grace on the other. The metaphor of the two levels, the heir of a long tradition which stretches from St Irenaeus to St Thomas, gives place to that of two different worlds between which there is no communication but rather conflict. In the political field the breakdown of thought is symbolized by the quarrel between the growing nation-states and the papacy. Victor Cousin was not wrong to sum up medieval history in three phases: in the first faith is predominant and reason subordinated; then faith and reason pursue parallel courses; finally the original relationship is reversed and reason, freed from any kind of dependence, wants to rule everything.

The final phase, however, is more complicated and incoherent than this scheme indicates. Nor must we jump to the conclusion that no useful work was done between the fourteenth and the sixteenth centuries. Decadence is a transition and transitions are fruitful. Three separate tendencies are to be observed in that period which are of the greatest importance for future syntheses: mystical union is boldly sought after, the human personality is taken seriously, and an attempt is made to detect the mechanical laws of the material universe. Will the future produce a synthesis to satisfy the new requirements? At any rate the notion of a Christian philosophy, something consciously accepted by civilization as a whole, is a dead notion which so far has not returned to life. Henceforth the individual must shoulder his own responsibilities and restore by his own free effort and in relative solitude that attitude of mind which was the nurse and mother of all for a thousand years. We shall find, no doubt, certain permanent lines of thought, but unanimity is no longer a matter of accepted fact; and even when philosophy is Christian it no longer derives from any widespread system of ideas.

CHAPTER IV

MODERN TIMES:
EXTREME POSITIONS

The early centuries of our era, as we have seen, Christianized Graeco-Roman ideas. St John's Logos is the first example, and the process is speeded up by the Alexandrian Fathers. When we read the obscure and impressive work of Marius Victorinus,◦ one of the first neo-Platonists to become a Christian, we receive the impression that the domestication of pagan concepts is proceeding at a dangerous pace and that the living God of the Gospel and the Person of Christ are becoming obscured by the proliferation of ideas associated with them. If there had been a large crop of writers like Marius Victorinus, or like John Scotus Erigena later on, one might have feared that Christian thought would collapse by reason of its own success, swamped by its own trophies.

On the other hand, there was practically no assimilation of the pagan gods and heroes. It is true that Orpheus is represented on Christian sarcophagi and in the paintings of the catacombs, where he prefigures the Good Shepherd. But the precise bearing of this adaptation is obscure, for we know too little about the nature of the Orphic religion if indeed there was such a thing. The first Christians probably believed that Orpheus was a historical personage like Socrates or one of the prophets, someone who had the privilege of discovering and of spreading faith in a single God because he had lived in Egypt where he had read the works of Moses. St Justin echoed this legend, and St Augustine takes the same line about Hermes Trismegistus. Occasionally the Fathers of the Church made favourable mention of the myth of Prometheus, saviour of men. But, apart from certain literary conventions, and these not accepted for some time, there is no indication of any considerable assimilation of the myths by Christian theology. For some Fathers, polytheism is simply a tissue of illusions due to the follies of mankind; for others, the gods exist, but they are really demons who pass themselves off as worthy of adoration.

That is the verdict on paganism until it has ceased to be a live issue. Then a different attitude is taken up and becomes normal. Euhemerus' interpretation, which makes the gods divinized heroes, now becomes popular, or the allegorizing theory of the Stoics according to which they are forces of nature. In the Middle Ages there were still hesitations about them, as indicated by the history of medicine: some related certain parts of the body to certain planets or to the signs of the Zodiac, others to patron saints. But, generally speaking, mythology belongs henceforth to the philosophical or artistic horizons of Christian people. It is no longer a manifestation of evil powers or a heresy. Isidore of Seville illustrates the point of view. Dante is quite explicit; the gods have a large part to play in his work; they are not only symbols of Platonic ideas but the equivalent of angels. Space is peopled with spirits who guide the stars and exert their influence on men. They are in the service of God, and we know this from Revelation: the ancients, having only their presentiments of the truth to guide them, identified these realities as best they could. The principle was a good one, as Beatrice explains to Dante in the fourth Canto of the *Paradiso*: but "misunderstood, it led astray the generality of the ancient world which spoke of Jupiter, Mercury and Mars". And Dante invoked Christ as the "supreme Jupiter" who was crucified for us. At this time the Sibyls appear in sculpture as pendants to the prophets. Without this humanist background Michelangelo's Sistine Chapel would be quite incomprehensible. The rehabilitation is not confined to literary or moral allegorism. A philosophy also undertakes it, which represents, at bottom, the extreme limit to which Christian philosophy has gone. This chapter has begun with a backward glance at the history of a certain line of thought—it had not been mentioned earlier for the simple reason that it leads up to and introduces our present concern: the extraordinary triumph of the extreme position known as the Renaissance. Far from being a return to paganism, the Renaissance is the final integration of paganism into Christianity and therefore a complete glorification of Christianity. *Latet sub fabula mysterium altius*,[1] declares the humanist Collucio Salutati in his *De laboribus Herculis*. Ronsard draws a parallel between the life of Hercules and that of Christ, the former having prepared the Gentiles for the coming of the latter.[2] Marsilius Ficinus, drawing upon Plato, welcomes the idea with enthusiasm. Pico della Mirandola, drawing upon hermetism, is clearly convinced *a priori* that the mythology and the wisdom of the Greeks carry with them an acknowledgement of Christ. Giordano Bruno ends his *Heroici Furori* with an allegorism which embraces both the physical world and humanity in quest of the Absolute.

The first impression of this exuberant epoch may be that, although Christianity is not denied, the thinkers of the sixteenth century are dwelling lovingly upon the beauties of creation rather than fixing their gaze upon the supernatural world. They have an insatiable thirst for facts. They want to "go places" and verify everything for themselves. Not only

---

[1] "A deeper mystery lies hidden beneath the fable."

[2] Quoted by M. Simon, *Hercule et le christianisme* (Paris, 1955), pp. 176 f. Ravaisson was thinking of this when he wrote: "People have tried to put Christianity back into mythology: we must put mythology back into Christianity."

are they interested, as the scholastics were, in the ideas or
the forces which make the world work, but they speculate
about the organisms and living spirits which make it up.
The work of God is illustrated, and the Creation reveals all
its splendour, precisely because it comes from God and bears
the mark of its divine origin. Man, as the centre of all
creatures, is so fine that he is unreservedly exalted and praise
is heaped upon him. To the theological reasons for his greatness, deriving from the Incarnation, others are now added of
a philosophical kind: man's freedom, his heroic self-affirma-
tion, the recapitulation on the human level of all the others.
Sometimes the two classes of reason, instead of lying parallel
one above the other, come together and coincide: for Nicholas
of Cusa, who leads the way in this respect, the great problem
is for man to become equal to himself, and he cannot do this
unless he finds his archetype realized in Christ. Anthropology
has something sacred and illimitable about it. It is this passion
for the human which explains the enthusiasm of scholars for
the past and the remote so as to store up every vibration of
man's soul. Then the material world suddenly lights up at
the touch of learned men, for whom Averroes and the Arabs,
rightly or wrongly, serve as a rallying-point. With Copernicus
or Christopher Columbus cosmic immensities, unguessed at
and irrefutable, come into view. The world seems to have
become infinite overnight. Some will affirm with Giordano
Bruno that it is literally so, and will go back to the Greek
atomists to justify belief in a plurality of worlds. But, even
in Giordano Bruno, even in the wildest excesses of humanism, is there really pantheism? It may be doubted. If the
reflection of God extends without limit, if the universe is one
and infinite, the greatness of God appears all the more un-
plumbable and overwhelming.

In this universe I posit a universal providence, in virtue of
which everything lives, grows, moves and endures in its perfection; and I conceive of it as acting in two ways, one being

the way in which the soul is present in the body, wholly, that is to say, and wholly in each part; the other being the ineffable way in which God, by his essence, his presence and his power, is in everything and above everything, not as a part, not as the soul, but inexplicably.[3]

This thinker, despite what has been said about him, does not absorb us in God; on the contrary, he describes in dramatic language the inability of man's mind to penetrate God's secret of itself, and the necessity of grace. The "heroic fury" of man is broken in a noble defeat before God's transcendence.

There is plenty of effervescence in this century; but the main stream of the Renaissance is an essentially Catholic phenomenon, a complement to patristic thought and to the authentic spirit of the Middle Ages.[4] That is why the notion of philosophy is still Christian, although the approach is not that of the twelfth or thirteenth century and although there are extravagances and a running to seed. The new scholasticism, too, that of Vittoria or Suarez, is very different from the old: turned rather towards the experience of this world, eager to find the foundations of a natural law for all races of mankind, it is humanist, scientific, ethical, without ceasing to be metaphysical. Everywhere men's minds are attracted by a new method, pervasive rather than explicitly formulated, in which formal deduction is less important than analysis and imagination. The community of individual beings under the eye of God and under the law of Christ is more interesting than the logic of abstract forms. Corresponding relationships are all the rage; the universal is no longer above individual things, but in their interdependence and their interaction.

[3] Quoted by P. H. Michel, introduction to G. Bruno, *Des fureurs héroïques* (Paris, 1954), pp. 28–9. Cf. p. 28: *Mens super omnia Deus est; mens insita omnibus natura; mens omnia pervadens ratio.*

[4] Here I accept the findings of G. Toffanin, *Storia del'Umanesimo*, Bologna, 1952, and believe myself not to be at variance with F. Hermans, *Histoire doctrinale de l'humanisme chrétien* (Tournai-Paris, 1948), I.

Nevertheless the sixteenth century is an unbalanced period. This is shown, for example, by the way in which it succumbs so readily to the attraction of demonology: Botticelli's angels shade off imperceptibly into demons. In Leonardo da Vinci and Michelangelo it is not so much a gradual transition as a terrifying alternation: a devil suddenly lets out a howl through the mouth of a Christian. Thus two sorts of immanence are found throughout the century, dividing men into two camps, sometimes making a division within one and the same man. At one extreme neo-pagans like Pomponazzi and the Averroists cut themselves off from Christianity altogether; but there are no more atheists than there were in previous centuries—rather there are more heretics, more seeds of atheism or scepticism scattered in many works which are moderate in their general tone, like Montaigne's Essays. In fine, it is an explosive period, ripe not for incredulity but for instability.

This lack of balance has another cause: the century produced, along with a Christian naturalism, a violent and complete rejection of it: the Reformation. In Luther and Calvin (if not in Zwingli, who was soaked in neo-Platonism) the notion of Christian philosophy is abolished at a stroke. Nature is corrupt; there is truth only in the Word of God which elects us and summons us to salvation. Apart from faith in Christ and in his sacrifice, there is no salvation and no sound principle. Reflection cannot save us; it is only one variety of servitude. The clash between the Reformation and the Renaissance is summed up in the contrast between Luther and Erasmus. The *De Servo Arbitrio* answers the *De libero arbitrio diatribe sive collatio* (published in 1524), and there is no sort of communication between the two. Eventually, it is true, the Reformation makes an important, if indirect, contribution to Christian philosophy, but at first and in principle it undermines the hopes of the humanists and drives them into the arms of the unbelievers and the dilettantes. Thus there is something of a return to the situation of the first centuries, for neo-Christians and neo-pagans have no longer any common ground. Even so there was more solidarity between the contending parties than in the past, since the biblicism of the Reformers and the philology of the humanists brought them together. Furthermore, between these extreme positions, there flowed both the vigorous current of Platonism and the broad stream of Jesuit scholasticism. All these schools flourished together and became interwoven like the threads in a piece of tapestry. Sometimes there were comical results: the Protestant universities of Germany were dominated by the scholasticism of Suarez, which supplanted the influence of Ramus and helped the Lutherans against the Arminian theologians of Heidelberg, who, within the Reformation movement itself, had taken up the cause of human liberty against an arbitrary predestinationism. It is indeed difficult for a religion to give up philosophy altogether; it requires a logic in order to express itself and in order to develop; but the logic developed a life of its own and brought back in its train a theory of knowledge and a metaphysic.

In general there was a passion for rather dubious ideas. The men of the Renaissance believed in various different sorts of finality, they dwelt upon concrete affinities and developed fascinating and extravagant hypotheses. The seventeenth century has the merit of diluting, and sometimes contradicting, the excessive optimism of the sixteenth. Without Descartes's critical genius the heritage of the Renaissance would have remained a chaos.

In a sense Descartes continues the work of his masters, the Jesuits of La Flèche; above all he follows the Augustinianism of his Oratorian friends. He is sincerely Christian, he accepts the experience of the inner life, he has faith in reason. Furthermore he develops the humanism of the learned world; he cultivates mathematics to the extent of giving his physics an overdose of it, he is persuaded, like Giordano Bruno, that the natural world is infinite, he peers into the secrets of nature, like Francis Bacon, with an indefatigable curiosity. But in another sense Descartes makes a completely fresh start, for he throws overboard three-quarters of the existing cargo. It is this relentless discrimination between the true and the false which is his strength. Methodical doubt and lucidity of judgement are the arms of this fearless warrior. He strips away much of the philosophical tradition, abolishes vague kinds of finality, makes a holocaust of the forms of the Scholastics, and replaces a tangled cosmology by a science of admirable simplicity. He achieves in some sort in philosophy that cleaning-up process which the Reformers wished to employ in the fields of dogma and liturgy. In the religious spheres he makes no profound changes; he thinks, like the Thomists, that philosophical inquiry is autonomous, but he bows to the verdict of Revelation. Whatever his audacities or his excesses elsewhere, he avoids them on this issue. He leaves theology aside as a rule, not because he despises it but because it is not his business.

Nor must we conclude that his tastes were exclusively profane, that he cheerfully dispensed with Jesus Christ in whom he had been baptized and was a Christian only by convention. Such a verdict might be justifiable if we had only the last pages of the *Discours de la Méthode* to go on, in which he describes a project for the renovation of mankind by mechanical means. But Descartes recovered that hunger for God which had never entirely left him. His writing on ethics, reminiscent of the Stoics, is punctuated by unmistakably sincere appeals to God. His metaphysic is hesitant about God's purposes, but he affirms their existence: "it does not seem that I could seek out and undertake to discover the impenetrable purposes of God without temerity." Descartes, at the end of his life at least, opens his mind more and more to religion; his faith is obscure and reticent, but perhaps intense, and there are certain luminous evidences. There is the extraordinary letter of February 1st, 1647, to Chanut, in which he denounces the extravagance of "loving only the divinity instead of loving God" and, after glorifying the Incarnation in terms which herald Pascal, nevertheless allows that we can love God by the power of our nature alone. "I do not maintain that this love is meritorious without grace, I leave that to the theologian to work out; but I venture to say that it is the most ravishing and most profitable passion that we can have; and indeed that it can be the strongest, although for that one needs to meditate very attentively, because we are continuously diverted by the presence of other objects." Descartes had a sense of balance. He put up a defence against anarchy, but it did not last. Hardly was the master dead when his system disintegrated. Everyone who kept a fragment of it supposed that he had the whole. The fascination of extreme positions was too strong and there were plenty of them to choose from—matter, science, reason, the self, all these great words had their worshippers who could claim Descartes' patronage. So could the worshippers of God: M. Emery, the superior of Saint-Sulpice in Napoleon's time, collected *Les Pensées de Descartes sur la religion et la morale*. At the opposite pole we may pass over at once his materialistic posterity, flourishing in the eighteenth century under Helvetius and La Mettrie, who were no doubt under the influence of other masters but who were only too glad to make use of the *Discours de la Méthode* in their attempt to reduce life to mechanism; we may also pass over the positivism of Auguste Comte, who believed himself to be continuing and perfecting the work of criticism begun two centuries earlier. It is all too clear that for such thinkers no Christian philosophy is possible, although they were obsessed by Christianity —they either attacked it or tried to neutralize it. Our business is rather with those successors of Descartes who recognized him as a "spiritual" philosopher. It will be easy enough to show that they departed from him very widely, consciously or otherwise. Furthermore, while all underwent his influence, they reacted to it in such a way that they differ endlessly among themselves.

The first of these antitheses is that between Descartes himself and Pascal. The whole of philosophy, according to Pascal, is not worth an hour's trouble. No doubt, by the "whole of philosophy" he means "the whole of physics", for the word had then a wider sense than it has today. But Pascal is passing judgement, sometimes at least, on the whole gamut of profane occupations, when he employs that process of alternating the arguments "for and against" which is a part of his method. He requires from his faith alone the principle of a universal synthesis, but he eliminates all *gnosis* from it, for he bases himself on experience and does not allow it to flatter his own desires. "I love poverty because Jesus Christ loved it"—this illuminating remark expresses the same experimental point of view as the theorems on atmospheric pressure or the statements about "the heart which realizes that there are three dimensions in space". If Pascal retains something of Descartes (e.g., the *cogito*, the infinite, etc.) he is very distrustful of the reason because it can be drawn in any direction by concupiscence. Here he is following St Augustine and Port Royal, with whom he shares not only his pessimism but also his passion for the divine Absolute.

The Christian philosophy which he offers us is in principle theirs; but it is original because it does not confine itself to requiring grace in order to safeguard the human mind. It has the great novelty of introducing the historical point of view into the search for truth. The true philosophy is identified with a study of historical events: the Creation, the Fall, the Redemption. St Justin spoke of testimony rather than of pure ideas, but in this he remained almost without a follower. Pascal is the first to echo him with any exactness. He is also the first to base himself on concrete existence, with its agonies, its hopes, its irreversible insertion into a time-process

of which Christ is the centre. Before faith has been accepted,
the analysis of the human condition, at once so great and so
wretched, gives rise to a philosophy, which is Christian
because the questions which spring from the fact of our own
existence find no satisfactory answer except in Christ.
Pascal's questioning and concrete thought both subjects the
material order to that of the soul and continues its analysis
in that order to show the soul's hazardous situation apart from
transcendent charity. Solitary and discontinuous, the world
of historical human beings is vowed to an absurd bankruptcy
unless Jesus has died to save it. Pascal begins and ends as a
theologian, but he conducts his analysis as a philosopher,
and in either case he thinks existentially; that is his innova-
tion.

The contrast between Descartes and Pascal is not complete,
but it is marked. The same is true in certain respects of other
pairs of thinkers: Spinoza, Leibniz, Hegel on one side, Malebranche, Kant, Kierkegaard on the other. It would take us
too far outside our subject to consider each of these antitheses in detail. A few characteristic quotations will be
enough to convince us that the Renaissance already contained
within it the germs of the various subsequent Christian philosophies. Spinoza, however, certainly cannot be considered a
Christian thinker, despite his admiration for Christ who
"conversed with God as spirit to spirit" and who did not hear
the voice of God like Moses but was himself the divine voice.
Malebranche's design, on the other hand, is to give a real
primacy to the Catholic faith: "Now that man's reason is enfeebled, it must be guided by authority." Malebranche begins
with Cartesian reason and pushes its rigorous arguments as
far as they will go; nevertheless his calm tone and limpid style
cannot deceive the attentive reader: he cannot base his teaching on reason, for he, like Pascal, comes up against the
limitations of our nature. M. Brunschwicg has even said that
Malebranche alone has built up a specifically Christian

philosophy. And M. Guéroult, referring to the combination in Malebranche of Augustinian vision and Cartesian analysis, has written that his teaching "cannot hold water without the implicit denial of what is supposed to be its one and only basis".[5]

His vision of things in the light of God and his occasionalism itself he claims to derive from a meditation on the faith. "God's first design was the Incarnation of his Son: it is for him that we were made, although he became incarnate for us". By putting the glory and the service of God above everything, this thinker has produced a philosophy of the divine Word in this world. But the grace which is called in to prop up the uncertain conclusions of natural reason seems sometimes an ambiguous affair. This provokes the sharp question whether Malebranche, by dint of supernaturalizing reason, has not rationalized grace. It depends on how one reads him. To identify reason with the Word is also to identify the Word with reason; to make attention the mind's natural prayer is either to transfigure attention or to evacuate prayer. M. Guéroult missed a point when he gave his verdict, for it is perhaps Malebranche's fate that he should lend himself to either of two logics, Pascal's or Spinoza's. He oscillates all the time between the extremes which he tries to surmount. Their coincidence is affirmed on the very first page of the *Traité de la nature et la grâce*: "A profane world was unworthy of God; God's wisdom made him, so to speak, incapable of acting in this way. Thus, on the supposition that God wishes to provide himself with an honour worthy of him (in which he is nevertheless wholly free, since he is perfectly sufficient to himself), then his wisdom in a sense fails unless it is itself first offered to him to be united to his work, since otherwise his work would not be worthy of him."

Leibniz leads us into different country. Like the Florentines Pico della Mirandola or Giordano Bruno, he exalts the created

[5] Malebranche, I, *La Vision en Dieu* (Paris, 1955), p. 311.

world and glorifies God's gifts in nature. But the emphasis is
on the acquisition of knowledge, and he who understands
the great truths is a mirror of the divine beauty.

> True love is founded on the knowledge of the beauty of the
> object loved. Now the beauty of God is seen in the wonderful
> effects of this sovereign cause. Thus, the more one knows of
> nature and of the solid truths of the physical sciences, which
> are rays of the divine perfection, the more can one truly love
> God. Jesus Christ having laid the foundations of the love of
> God by that knowledge alone which is common to all men, it
> is for us to strengthen these great notions day after day by
> the fresh natural lights which God has given us expressly for
> that purpose and of which grace makes use according to each
> one's disposition.

To put on Christ, "according to the disposition" of Leibniz, is
to hate non-being and to adhere to the origin of our existence;
but it is not at all to hate oneself and to empty oneself so as
to make room for God, as Fénelon would have it. Let us
recollect ourselves, but let us not fall into lethargy. "The
annihilation of what properly belongs to us, which is pushed
very far by the quietists, might well be a form of disguised
impiety on the part of certain persons."

The philosophy of Leibniz is Christian because it binds up
Christianity with universal knowledge. He offers an "eternal
philosophy", following up an idea which was already familiar
to the men of the Renaissance and giving it a more scientific
turn. One of the first writers to use the expression, Steuco
(in his book *De perenni philosophia*), claimed that Christian
dogmas, and in particular that of the Trinity, were to be
found in Plato and the neo-Platonists. In some respects the
point of view is still to be met with, in our own time, in
Simone Weil's *La Source grecque*. Revelation is diffused and
overflows into the religious insight granted to the sages of
all times and countries. Thus to say that philosophy is

Christian would be to point to the source both of its unity and of its stability.

Kant entirely contradicts Leibniz's rational optimism. He sides with Luther; that is to say, he philosophizes in order to show the insufficiency of philosophy. It is impossible for the reason to attain to things in themselves, things as they really are. The existence of God itself is undemonstrable; it is admitted only as a postulate of the practical reason. The idea of God is based upon duty, the sense of obligation, but duty is not based on the idea of God—it is founded on itself in so far as it is identified with the reason. Kant considers that he must "suppress knowledge so as to leave room for belief". The life of religion is reduced to morality; it can be only a corollary of a pure sense of duty, that is to say, of a disposition to act according to a universally valid rule, independent of all empirical content and of all sentimental impulse, for man's sensibility is corrupt. So the norm of conduct is to perform one's actions in such a way that no contradiction is implied. And the norm of religion is to believe what is compatible with such actions. The only way of honouring God properly is to live morally. Kant subjects the dogmas and rites of the Churches to severe criticism; he finds in them unacceptable anthropomorphisms. Prayer is very antipathetic to him: doesn't it presuppose the mentality of a courtier who flatters his prince out of self-interest?

What becomes of the Christian Revelation in such a context? Kant reduces it to his categorical imperative, and it is in this spirit that he writes his thesis "on religion within the limits of reason". He tells us that "it is not essential nor therefore necessary for us to know what God can do or could have done for our salvation, but only to know what we hope to do ourselves so as to deserve his help". This declaration of indifference is clear enough. Nevertheless Kant makes ingenious efforts to give Holy Scripture and the articles of the Creed a rational sense. These are for him the "mystic

envelopes" which have served to make moral truths accessible
to the generality. He venerates them in theory and eliminates
them in practice. But we must not conclude that this religious
philosophy is anti-Christian. It can defend itself from the
charge for good reasons. In the first place it acknowledges
that reason itself is mysterious; it forbids us to suppose that
we can adequately penetrate the revelation which is immanent
in the reason. Again Kant is not wrong to require that Revelation should be compatible with a maximum of intelligibility.
Lastly, he understood more and more as he grew older that
the "envelope" was indispensable, and in his last writings he
has even shown more sympathy for the positive content of the
Bible and the person of Jesus. But if he had admitted that
there could be a Christian philosophy, he would have understood it quite differently from Leibniz. These two thinkers
of the Enlightenment are as far as possible removed from one
another, except in their exaltation of personal dignity and the
moral life. The illuminism of the one may be fairly identified
with Christian wisdom: the illusionism of the other sees in
revealed truth only a darkness to dissipate, and he makes a
violent separation between knowledge and faith within the
life of the mind.

Hegel's philosophy is indebted to Leibniz, but he brings
God more into the world. Christianity is completely annexed
by his speculations. Philosophy is the history of humanity
in so far as it thinks and judges itself in the unfolding of
its mental processes. And the Christian fact has an importance which Hegel seizes upon and places unhesitatingly in
the centre of the picture. It would be fantastic to refuse his
philosophy the epithet "Christian" when it proves to contain
so many brilliant aphorisms about the redemptive Incarnation and the Trinity.

God is thus recognized as *Spirit* only when known as the
Triune. This new principle is the axis on which the History

of the World turns. This is *the goal* and the *starting point* of History. "When the fullness of time was come, God sent his son", is the statement of the Bible. . . . *Christ has appeared—a Man who is God—God who is Man; and thereby peace and reconciliation have accrued to the World. . . . That natural elation of soul which characterized the Greeks did not rise to the Subjective Freedom of the Ego itself—to the inwardness that belongs to the Christian Religion—to the recognition of Spirit as a definite positive being.* The appearance of the Christian God involves further its being *unique* in its kind; it can occur only once, for God is realized as Subject, and as manifested Subjectivity is exclusively One Individual. The Lamas are ever and anon chosen anew; because God is known in the East as Substance, whose infinity of form is recognized merely in an unlimited multeity of outward and particular manifestations. But subjectivity as infinite relation to self, has its form *in itself*, and, as manifested, must be a unity excluding all others.[6]

Kierkegaard has nothing but sarcasm for this dialectic in which everything works out necessarily in the development of a too human Absolute. As Kant opposed Leibniz, so the Danish thinker opposes Hegel. Christian philosophy undergoes yet another metamorphosis: this time we have the extreme case of an existential despair in which reason, driven to faith, repudiates philosophy. Life is solitude, anguish, a fearful choice. No rational norm holds good in face of that exception which is the individual's destiny. To escape into the world of art or to make generalizations about morality is always to shirk the real personal problem. On the other hand, the faith of Abraham or of Job shirks nothing, but for immediate experience and for learned reflection it is a scandal and its promises are absurd, for it is necessary to hand oneself over to Christ the Saviour and to make oneself the contemporary of his sacrifice. Is there still a philosophy in this world-

[6] *Lectures on the Philosophy of History* by G. W. F. Hegel (Eng. Trans., London, 1861), p. 331, 336–7.

vision racked by paradox where reason is declared bankrupt from the start? If so, it cannot be formulated. If one may speak of choosing Christianity and of thought which justifies the choice, this thought is not justified itself by essences but by bitter experience. In his Journal Kierkegaard declares:

> Philosophy and Christianity can never be united. For if, however little it may be, I am to maintain what is the very essence of Christianity, namely the Redemption, it must naturally extend, if it is real, over the whole life of man. I might be able to imagine a philosophy after Christianity, or after a man has become a Christian. But that will be a Christian philosophy. In its highest accomplishment, philosophy would involve its own total ruin, that is, it would make plain that it cannot fulfil its original intention.[7]

Liberty is ballasted by anguish, and wisdom jettisoned by faith. Nevertheless there is a concealed logic in this drama, that of personal vocation and of its fulfilment. Kierkegaard, who had a regard for Socrates and a certain tolerance for Descartes, at least admitted that "the exception once established is reconciled with the general rule".

About the same time other Christians, belonging to the Catholic obedience, were making light of the individual. These were the traditionalists, in whom we find two strains of thought. On the one hand, de Bonald, J. de Maistre and Lamennais relentlessly denounce the insufficiency of the individual reason, and Bautain depreciated the intellect even more than his master Kant. On the other hand, the traditionalists claim to know everything: they believe themselves to be in possession of a universal science and they would be ashamed to be mere specialists. They are unwittingly men of the Renaissance. This apparent contradiction is ingeniously resolved by their faith in a primitive revelation of God to

[7] Quoted by R. Jolivet, *Introduction to Kierkegaard* (Eng. Trans., London, 1950), p. 95.

humanity. Speech itself is a gift from heaven to Adam, and thought is simply a higher form of language handed down from generation to generation. Spiritual certainties, therefore, are always founded on a tradition. Thus the *gnosis* and the agnosticism of these thinkers are made compatible with one another. But the original tradition which communicated to men the mysteries of the divine life has been broken into fragments in course of time. The religion and philosophy of the pagans are the elements, now unrecognizable, of a shattered synthesis. The task of modern philosophy must be, aided by the history of civilization, to reconstruct this lost totality. When the pieces of the broken mirror have been reassembled, the face of God will at once appear therein, for our knowledge will have recaptured the primitive revelation and detected the meaning of the Judaeo-Christian revelation. Thus traditionalism has the glorification of Christ as its ideal, a certain esotericism as its inspiration, and an encyclopaedic effort as the means of its realization. Its philosophy is Christian and in a complex way: truth is a grace brought to us by the authority of a prophet and not by the thought of a critical philosopher; this truth is nothing but the emanation of a personal God, transmitted by human persons down the centuries; it is historical, and yet it is expressed eventually in a coherent system of affirmations. Jesus Christ, who restored the old Adam to his original dignity, is the living centre from whom all the ideas of universal wisdom are derived in their entirety. Every race, pagan or Christian, has brought its tribute to this source, and this both forced eclecticism upon the traditionalists and gave them credit in the eyes of their contemporaries, for the end of the eighteenth century and the beginning of the nineteenth identified eclecticism with philosophy.

Many other forms of Christian philosophy might be examined. Secrétan begins with the divine liberty as a regulative hypothesis given to us by faith; he deduces from it the whole economy of the universe. He attaches a metaphysical structure, conditionally, to a theological thesis. Nearer to our own time, William James and, above all, Bergson reason in a completely opposite direction: the Christian fact or mystical experience are accepted by them as data and they subject them to critical experiment. They conclude that the witness of believers is sound and that it passes their tests. So they incorporate Christianity into their philosophy by way of induction. Their method undoubtedly proves that metaphysics today is considered to be inseparable from concrete facts and that its programme contains a historical element. This would certainly not rejoice the shade of Aristotle. In a sense, it is a victory for Hegel.

I have not tried to paint a complete picture of an epoch; I have only taken examples. But the impression which results from these few pages is a definite one: modern times do not present us with a homogeneous concept of Christian philosophy. The upshot of the inquiry is bewildering; no common measure has been found, and this disharmony casts doubt on the intelligibility of such a concept. Has this Proteus any substance? Are its evolutions a sign of poverty or of wealth? Inevitably the minds of philosophers were disturbed by this situation, and the very possibility of a Christian philosophy became the subject of a debate. The astonishing thing is that this inquiry, which we must now examine in detail, did not open before 1931.

PART II

THE RECENT DEBATE AND ITS RESULTS

CHAPTER V

THE DEBATE OF 1931

Our century was certainly not the first to apply the epithet "Christian" to philosophy in a more than casual fashion. For instance, André Martin, a seventeenth-century Oratorian, composed, under the name of Ambrosius Victor, a *Philosophia Christiana*, which, in fact, is nothing more than a collection of texts from St Augustine. It is not so easy to find *histories* of Christian philosophy, that is, treatises which expound its diverse forms without making it their main object to justify one of them at all costs. Such productions belong, apparently, only to the nineteenth century; there was Henri Ritter's in 1843, Ozanam's in 1855. And the only *critical examination* of the idea itself was perhaps that of the German C. J. Branis, a work of considerable penetration.[1] The debate of 1931, to which we shall now turn, was thus, in effect, a beginning, strange as this may seem.

In 1928 M. Emile Bréhier had delivered three lectures in Brussels entitled "Is there a Christian Philosophy?". His answer was that there was not. Prof. Etienne Gilson promptly took up the challenge and opened a discussion in the *Société française de philosophie* on March 21st, 1931. He began by asking whether the idea has meaning, and the summary of his reply is as follows:

> The question can be answered in the affirmative if we treat the problem as a historical one. We have then to decide whether

[1] *De notione philosophiae christianae* (Breslau, 1825).

Christianity has in fact played a visible part in the formation of certain philosophies. If we find philosophical systems, purely rational in their principles and methods, which could not have come into existence without the Christian religion, then the philosophies thus defined deserve to be called Christian. This notion does not correspond to a pure essence, that of a philosopher or that of a Christian, but to the possibility of a complex historical reality, that of a revelation which is productive of human reasoning. The two orders remain distinct, although the relationship which unites them is an intrinsic one.[2]

Elaborating this notion, Gilson writes:

A philosophy open to the supernatural would certainly be compatible with Christianity, but it would not necessarily be a Christian philosophy. If it is to deserve that name, the supernatural must descend as a constitutive element not, of course, into its texture, which would be a contradiction, but into the work of its construction. Thus I call Christian *every philosophy which, although keeping the two orders formally distinct, nevertheless considers the Christian revelation as an indispensable auxiliary to reason.*[3]

Thus philosophies are Christian if they undergo the influence of revelation as the result of a deliberate attitude of mind on the part of their authors. They presuppose a certain choice of problems, for they bear upon the religious aspect of philosophy: "God, man in his relations with God, nature in its relations with God." But, concentrated on God as they are, they will have to engross all that is necessary for a synthesis, and in this sense they will not be limited to metaphysics, anthropology and ethics, which form the kernel of them.

In the session of 1931 M. Gilson considered only a theoreti-

[2] *Bulletin de la Société française de philosophie*, 31st year (1931), p. 39.
[3] *The Spirit of Mediaeval Philosophy* (Gifford Lectures, 1931–2). London, 1936, p. 37.

cal and preliminary problem. The exchanges which followed
led him, quite naturally, to change the angle of his approach
and to speak as a historian: he asked nothing better! His
reply was only to be expected: Christian philosophy is not
only a possibility but a reality; it is realized not only in the
philosophy of St Thomas, but also in those of St Augustine,
St Bonaventure and Duns Scotus. Its forms are multiple, and
it would be arbitrary to reduce them to a unity. What unites
Christian philosophers is their faith: it puts them into a position intrinsically different from that of unbelievers, for their
reason knows what it is trying to demonstrate; and, as
Leo XIII put it in one of his Encyclicals, it has a "guiding
star".

The author vigorously denounces the idea that a philosopher can think independently of his religious convictions.
There is a way of separating natural speculation from faith
which is an absurd pretence. Gilson is also keenly aware (and
he became more and more keenly aware) of the feebleness
of reason left to its own resources. As a psychologist and a
historian, he points to the fumblings and the follies of the
human mind. Fundamentally, he has little confidence in the
autonomous powers of the intellect. I would almost say (but
this might be an exaggeration) that he is in that respect a
Jansenist; he believes in the history of philosophy much more
than in philosophy. Without grace, what mistakes men make,
without revelation what Towers of Babel are constructed!

In his Gifford Lectures he develops this thesis in the following way:

1. Greek philosophy, despite its exceptional strength, never
succeeded in reaching monotheism: "we find no Greek philosophical system which has reserved the name of God for a
unique being and has suspended on the notion of such a God
the whole system of the Universe." M. Gilson has no great
difficulty in convincing us that, in Aristotle's eyes, pure
actuality and uncreated necessity are not the apanage of a

unique Being, the creative cause of the Universe. Instead of
a single unmoved mover, peripatetic metaphysics admits
forty-seven or fifty-five: "Aristotle's polytheism prevented
him from conceiving of the divine as any other than the
attribute of a class of beings." But when he proposes to
banish God from Platonic philosophy the enterprise is a less
simple one. M. Gilson found himself opposed by scholars
like A. E. Taylor (and he would find still more of them today).
So in his closing lectures he seems anxious to recognize that
Plato in other contexts, for instance in discussing the inwardness of the moral law, showed himself "as near to Christianity
as one can be without being a Christian". In any case it is a
striking fact that M. Gilson is more severe to Greek theodicy
than Père Laberthonnière had been. The latter, who re-
proached scholasticism for admitting more Aristotelian than
evangelical doctrine into its system, did not deny that there
was monotheism among the Greeks but only that its spirit was
akin to that of Christians.

2. The Middle Ages, M. Gilson continues (departing still
further from Père Laberthonnière's position), added a depth
to ancient philosophy of which the latter seems to have had
no inkling; the scholastics, helped by their faith, pressed the
principles of Hellenic thought to conclusions which the Greeks
had not in any way suspected. Thus St Thomas knows perfectly well that Aristotle did not teach the doctrine of creation,
but "what he is concerned to discover and to demonstrate is
that, although Aristotle had no awareness of this capital truth,
his principles, as they stand, are nevertheless capable of sup-
porting it". Faith was thus morally necessary for the progress
and the accuracy of a religious philosophy in the natural
order. Mgr Jolivet has developed a similar thesis on the subject with much brilliance, and M. Gilson's arguments are
very powerful. He is careful not to underrate the wisdom of
the ancients or to suppose it incapable of entering into a
more perfect synthesis. He shows himself to be as generously

humanistic as he is resolutely Christian. With much subtlety
and insight he perceives that a similarity of language between
Thomist thinkers and those of the ancient world conceals a
fundamental difference; there is a Christian content beneath
the vocabulary of Plato and Aristotle which gives it a wholly
new significance. The greatness of scholasticism lies in its
gentle refashioning of old formulas in such a way as to dis-
turb as little as possible their well-ordered structure. It is true
that this metamorphosis presupposes not only a more supple
form of reasoning but also new principles of thought, and
M. Gilson, I think, would be the first to recognize this. The
materials provided by the Greeks were excellent. Yet was it
sufficient, in order to build a Christian edifice, to add to the
uncompleted temple of wisdom an extra arch or to complete
the peristyle? It is the architecture itself which must be re-
fashioned, and the danger, today as in the Middle Ages, is
always to forget this fundamental condition.

3. "There is but one God and this God is Being: that is
the corner-stone of all Christian philosophy; and it was not
Plato, it was not even Aristotle, it was Moses who put it
in position."[4] The allusion is to Yahweh's utterance in
Exodus: "I am who am."[5] From this sacred text and from
the patristic commentaries on it M. Gilson draws many consequences, some of them surprising. God alone is complete
Being, self-sufficient; essence and existence, identical in him,
are distinct everywhere else. He is transcendent in regard to
the world, which is a free creation of his omnipotence; the
world of changing things is utterly dependent upon the
immutable plenitude of the Eternal. Infinite Being is the end
to which all things move, and this is the principle of Christian
optimism. The moral law, which is now a perfectly inward

[4] *Op. cit.*, p. 51.
[5] The exegete might point out that in Hebrew the exact sense of
the passage is rather: "I am who I am." God refuses to define himself
by revealing his name, and we cannot penetrate his mystery. Even
if the traditional translation is accepted, the reply seems rather evasive.

affair at bottom, is based on the transcendence of a sovereign Good. Human personality, which participates in the divine mind, gains an incomparable dignity: "in the act of bringing chance under law" Christian philosophy "frees nature from Fate".[6]

The metaphysics of love, the author concludes, is "wholly based . . . on the metaphysics of being".[7] This may well seem a bold statement, and its force is somewhat weakened by this concluding passage: "Philosophy, by virtue of the fact that it is a rational science, tends to unity; religious mysteries, although they act upon it, are not incorporated into it; the religious influence of the Gospel controls it from a further height by reason of its very profundity. That is why Christian philosophy may appear both richer than others and, at the same time, poorer than others in regard to the religion which nourishes it."

So definite an attitude could not fail to raise doubts. After all did Christianity succeed in bringing into philosophy only a doctrine of being which is more Jewish than evangelical? And isn't the doctrine itself the Aristotelian doctrine of pure act? Should we call Christian a doctrine which is rigidly confined to absolute existence? Moreover in a subsequent volume called *Christianisme et Philosophie* M. Gilson, although maintaining that philosophy is not theology, allowed that "the phrase 'Christian philosophy' and even the very notion of it express a theological view of philosophy". Isn't all that somewhat disturbing? So M. Gilson, if he could claim numerous supporters, including Prof. Maritain, found himself faced by some objections.

The most radical of them was Emile Bréhier's. If by Christian philosophy, he said, we mean a philosophy which is in accordance with dogma and which ecclesiastical authority

[6] *Op. cit.*, p. 371.
[7] *Op. cit.*, p. 277.

declares to be such, then the description is a theological one.
The attitude of authority may vary with the centuries: thus
the Church required Descartes to reconcile his theory of
matter with the dogma of the Real Presence, although it
addresses no such demands to modern physicists. But the
decisions of religious authorities, whether lenient or severe,
concern them only. Thus understood, Christian philosophy is
a historical fact, and its existence is undoubted: but it does
not in any way concern philosophy as such.

Another sense in which the expression may be used does,
however, concern philosophy directly: in this sense a
"Christian philosophy" is one which finds its origin in revelation. M. Bréhier believes that history cannot show us an
instance of it. In the early days of Christianity the Greek
world had a doctrine of the Logos, that is, of a rational
power which relates the world and the human spirit to the
divine. The Christians took over this notion, but they substituted for its rational content "a mysterious history of the
relations of God with man, a mysterious history which can
only be revealed". Thus we have on the one side a rationalism
and on the other a faith in the authority of a witness. These
are two attitudes of mind which have no common measure.
When St Augustine said that he had found in Plato the Eternal
Word but not the Word Incarnate, he drew the boundary line
very clearly and made his own choice. He remembers his
Plato, but he does not amalgamate Plato with the Gospel, and
he does not extract from the latter a philosophy. With St
Thomas Aquinas, there is an explicit juxtaposition of philosophy and dogma, Aristotle supplying the former and
Christianity containing the latter. But since, when there is a
collision between them, faith tells one what is true, philosophy
has only an illusory autonomy: it is controlled by dogma and
must at once give way to its complaints. Rationalism is practically turned out of its own house, all the more so because a

miracle can upset the natural stability of things. The two elements cannot be bound up together.

M. Bréhier deals with his other examples on the same principle. Descartes, personally, had the Christian faith, but it had no effect on his speculation, which depended upon itself alone. The traditionalism of the nineteenth century has obviously nothing to do with philosophy, since it despaired of critical reflection. Its real purpose was to ensure social order, so that Auguste Comte could even get rid of the dogmatic element and retain nothing of religion except its conservatism. If we go on to the last resurrection of this alleged "Christian philosophy", Maurice Blondel's *l'Action*, we find that it is in part the continuation of a very old philosophical inquiry about human happiness. Blondel examines human nature by the method which the Greeks had initiated. It is true that he does not look for inward peace where Epicurus and the Stoics found it. But that is because he adds to his philosophy of will an apologetic for belief, which is something quite different: the junction between the two is an accidental one. In short "one can no more speak of a Christian philosophy than of a Christian mathematics or a Christian physics".

Léon Brunschwicg has a similar point of view. "I should not recognize myself", he honestly declares, "in my thoughts and in my feelings if the whole Christian movement had never occurred." But does this indebtedness affect the structure of philosophy? "There is no point in examining the notion of Christian philosophy unless one interposes an adverb between the noun and the adjective, and no doubt somebody will at once say that the devil is appearing in the guise of a grammarian. I say, then, that for me the problem is that of a *specifically* Christian philosophy." There was a desire to baptize Aristotle; but he did not ask to be baptized, and he remains irreducibly pagan. Furthermore, M. Brunschwicg has no more indulgence for him than for St Thomas, for their attachment to the judgement of attribution is, in his eyes, the

mark of a puerile method in philosophy. Only the judgement
of relation, of which mathematics offers us the model, can
establish or express a philosophy which will hold water in our
century. We must seek for a spiritual unity by shedding all
egoism and renouncing all transcendence so that there may be
formed in us a reason which is eager to understand the world
according to its objective laws. We must choose between
Pascal and Spinoza, between sacred history and purely
rational reflection. That is Brunschwicg's conclusion.

The debate in the *Société de philosophie* caused considerable repercussions. In the Review of the faculty of Protestant theology at Strasbourg, M. Pierre Guérin pronounced
himself in favour of separating the two domains. "The more
a God is known, the less he is adored", he wrote. The
mind wants to possess the truth, the soul to give itself to the
religious object. Hence faith and critical reflection are, in a
sense, in inverse ratio. Christian philosophy is a bastard product which endangers both the purity of Christianity and the
autonomy of philosophy. It is easy to realize this if we look
at scholasticism, against which M. Guérin repeats a good
many of Laberthonnière's criticisms. All that is desirable is a
religious phenomenology which neither affirms nor denies
anything, confining itself to an understanding of the religious
object in the way in which one examines a work of art, extract-
ing its aesthetic value without any desire to impose the
analysis as though it were a part of the work of art itself.
The "philosophy of Christianity" would not have the draw-
backs of a "Christian philosophy". Towards the end of his
penetrating article the author admits that the expulsion of the
intellectual element from religion might encourage illusions
and that religion requires inevitably a certain reclothing in
ideas. He sees in this drawing together of reason and faith a
tension and a paradox imposed on us by life in this world;
the Incarnation of the Word contained the mystery already
and is its prototype. Let intelligence be present to faith by

all means—but if it represents faith to itself equivocation begins. Even if a representation of this sort is inevitable, it needs to be watched. Theology is legitimate, but it is dangerous; when a concept offers its services it may easily turn into a tyrant. That is why Christian philosophies have been sometimes crypto-theologies, which concealed their real postulates, sometimes insidious profanations which enervate faith.

In 1933 the Thomist Society of France put on its programme the topic discussed in Paris. This was the origin of a meeting at Juvisy in which divergences of opinion came to light. It is noteworthy that the neo-scholastics of Louvain who were present at this symposium were among those who declared on the whole against the possibility of a Christian philosophy in the strict sense. Prof. van Steenberghen laid it down clearly that a Christian, without renouncing his faith and even while gaining material inspiration from it, can and should abstract from his faith when he is conducting a critique of natural knowledge. If the influence of revealed data on speculation is intrinsic, then we are dealing with theology: if it is extrinsic or simply psychological, we cannot conclude to the existence of a Christian philosophy. "Philosophy and theology indicate two directions, one rising upwards to God, the other coming down from him: it is impossible for a third direction to be both at the same time, to be both a rational philosophy and a Christian one."[1]

Maurice Blondel's reaction to these various views was not long delayed. Although he had been unable to attend the meeting in Paris he sent a long letter which expressed his mind on the matter, and it was published along with the report of the debate. Not long after appeared his book *Le Problème de la philosophie catholique* in which the whole subject was considered afresh.

[1] I borrow this summary from A. Renard's excellent book, *La Querelle sur la possibilité de la philosophie chrétienne* (Paris, 1941), p. 33.

We should be grateful, he considered, to E. Bréhier for defending the purity and the rigour of rational thought: nothing is more insupportable than certain Christian philosophies whose hybrid and inconsistent character he justly denounced. But Bréhier opposes an excessively static view of the reason to a capricious view of revelation; these are "two caricatures": "I am no less surprised at what is offered to us as pure and perfect rational speculation among the Greeks than at what is presented to us under the name of Christianity." Blondel further defended himself from the charge of yielding to an apologetic prejudice, since *l'Action* stops at the threshold of the temple and keeps clear throughout of the conclusion from which it is accused of starting. Finally he protests vigorously against the analogy with a Christian mathematics with which Bréhier seeks to disqualify a Christian philosophy. The two cases are entirely different. A particular science can by no means be assimilated to that total reflection upon our concrete condition which is the business of philosophy.

But the most vigorous replies are addressed to M. Gilson, and this is at first surprising. Blondel absolutely refuses to settle the problem of Christian philosophy on the ground of history, and he reproaches Gilson for having done so. Two presuppositions, he says, have vitiated the inquiry: first, there is the idea that a philosophy tends normally to become a closed system; secondly, there is a sort of concordism which is equally injurious to philosophy and to Christianity, for in order to make revelation productive of rational systems it robs it of its supernatural character, and this involves the presupposition that philosophy can absorb the revealed data without having first discovered its own insufficiency—that is indispensable if the supernaturality of these data is to be preserved intact. History would be, in Gilson's view, the crucible in which faith and reason achieve a transmutation, but Blondel believes that in fact Gilson introduces a foreign body into the rational framework and so deprives it of its legitimate autonomy. The method which consists in sorting out the affinities which are common to philosophers and to believers (such as the existence of God and the creation of the world) loses sight of the fact that the perspectives of philosophy and of faith are not the same.

The way in which Christianity acts upon philosophy is quite different: it obliges philosophy to make fresh starts, and it helps it to become aware of its congenital insufficiency. We might put this more directly and more precisely by saying that for Blondel true philosophy is the mind's autonomous discovery of the inevitably incomplete character which attaches to all rational undertakings and in particular to all philosophic systematizations. This "void" is "no chimerical fiction, no projection, disquiet or disease of the soul; it has, if one may so put it, contours which can be discerned, an explanation to be considered and to be made rationally acceptable, a power of attraction and command, but one which we must not give way to by losing our heads or losing our right to gaze at this abyss. . . ."

Isn't this a profound and complicated way of coming back to Pascal's conclusion that "the final stage of reason is to recognize that there is an infinity of things which surpass it"? Blondel's thesis, however, is much more precise and much bolder: for the acknowledgement of insufficiency is equivalent to the discovery of a need, inevitable for reflection but inefficacious, of supernatural life, that is, of a state which is not only transcendent but superior to all the capacities of any creature whatsoever. Religious philosophy, then, must indicate the place at which the supernatural, if there is one, is to be inserted. It can neither evade the hypothesis of the necessity of the supernatural nor itself supply it. There is no "separated philosophy", but neither is there a watered-down philosophy or a *via media* between philosophy and theology. Blondel's famous statement that he has made "an attempt to philosophize as a believer" is clarified by another formula of his: "heterogeneity in compenetration and symbiosis in incommensurability". Reason must try to be in some sort coextensive with everything that is presented to it, including the data of revelation; but it does not attain to these except in the perspective of its self-limitation.

The voice of nature which groans in our nature itself forbids us to stop at a separated philosophy or a natural religion; it obliges us, on the other hand, to make our reflection a reply which implores the grace of God. But this is never a yielding to anything except a deliberate desire for complete sincerity. Any philosophy which reaches this point is a Christian one. With a sort of hypothetical ultimatum it signifies to us that we should have to accept the supernatural if it were proposed to us: it further signifies to us the conditions of its reception and of its assimilation by critical thought in such a case. The option itself, the adhesion of faith, is something beyond philosophical activity and cannot therefore be confused with it.

Blondel refers to Christian philosophy in the singular, meaning by this a spirit rather than a definite manifestation of it, attached to a particular school. Indeed he prefers to speak of "Catholic philosophy" because the term seems to him both "more comprehensive and more restrictive, since on the one hand it is applicable to men of good faith who participate in the grace (even if unrecognized) and the soul of the invisible Church, and since on the other hand Catholicism is alone able to specify what is supernaturally Christian". Thus the interlocking of faith and reason is given the maximum clarity of definition, without making the latter do anything but its proper rational business, by indicating the void which can be filled by revelation.

The same anxiety to respect the heterogeneity of the two domains, and to recognize nevertheless the secret aspiration with which man's reflections on himself and on the world is shot through, has inspired Professor Roger Mehl's subtle and rewarding book, *La Condition du philosophe chrétien*.[8] He quotes Lachelier's remark: "It is the duty of philosophy to comprehend everything, even religion." Like Lachelier and Blondel, and even more than they, he insists that this duty is never completely realized but remains subject to an end which evades its grasp: philosophy is eschatological. Lachelier thought that its function was to purify the Christian by a critical ascesis. M. Mehl urges, correlatively, that faith should incite philosophy to an unceasing conversion. His eyes are fixed on the Christian philosopher much more than on Christian philosophy; the latter has been too often vitiated by a deplorable eclecticism, or else it reflects theology and becomes its slave; the former, however, exists and has the right to exist, although his condition is a difficult one. "Let us not give the name of Christian to a philosophy which utilizes Christian data or even just Christian suggestions, for such a philosophy can remain profoundly pagan; but let us call Christian the philosophy of a man who knows that the Kingdom is near at hand, that all things are to become new, and who prepares himself, in philosophical reflection, for the coming of this Kingdom. . . ." A spirit and not a series of theses, an orientation and not an essence—that is what M. Mehl derives from Blondel, always referring to "the existential condition of the Christian philosopher", and refusing to give God a place in a beatified ontology which would degrade the mystery—an attitude which is not unlike that of Gabriel Marcel.

More recently M. Claude Tresmontant has, if I may so put it, given Blondelianism a twist in a different direction. In his work the affirmation of insufficiency is swallowed up by the joy of renewal. For Mehl, Christian philosophy is a soul in search of a body, and it can be embodied, provisionally, everywhere. For Tresmontant, on the contrary, it is a body of determined and well-articulated truths. An elect race of

[8] Neuchâtel, 1947.

Semites, acting as the instrument of God, has brought these into the world for the destruction of every *gnosis*. "The philosophical requirements of Christianity" is the title of one of Blondel's last works. Tresmontant undertakes to provide a list of them and to oppose Biblical metaphysics to those of India or Greece. Thus creation, the non-eternity of the world, transcendence and the personality of God are incompatible with those categories of the Hellenic world which are breaking up at all points today and are as ill-adapted to modern physics as they are to Christian faith. Blondel found that Athene's forehead had been enlarged in the last two thousand years. Tresmontant, less benignly, would not mind saying that Athene's forehead is too narrow, and he would attend the obsequies of the grey-eyed goddess and of her logic without shedding a tear. No doubt he would praise her for having loved contemplation, but his funeral speech would go no further than that.

CHAPTER VI

THE EXISTING OPTIONS

The simplest option is the following: there is no Christian philosophy, never has been and never will be, because the very idea is unthinkable. We have heard Emile Bréhier's pronouncement in this sense and the applause which greeted it from several Thomists who were nevertheless philosophers of a very different kind. But isn't this too simple an attitude? Blondel had no difficulty in pointing out to Bréhier that philosophy engages the whole man and is not limited to a special field like geometry or medicine, while Gilson explained: "Why do certain neo-scholastics suppose that their philosophy, even when controlled by theology, remains identical in its nature with one which recognizes no wisdom above itself?"

In this chapter I shall allow that the idea of Christian philosophy has a meaning. Yet the metamorphoses which it has undergone and the controversies which it has aroused are enough to show plainly that the meaning is far from clear. I shall therefore try to make it less obscure and with that purpose to classify the principal meanings which we have come across or which we could conceive of *a priori*. We are at a cross-roads. What are the possible directions? Let us draw a map of the district so as to make a well-informed choice.

1. The first possible direction is represented by the formula: *A Christian philosophy is one which prepares for or heralds Christianity*. "I advise you", Origen once wrote to Gregory

the Wonderworker, "to use as a propaedeutic for Christianity the philosophy of the Greeks and any datum of geometry or astronomy which can help with the exegesis of Sacred Scripture." Thus the Alexandrians were only taking up again the idea which had filled the mind of Justin. But what does this mean? If the connection between philosophy and faith is no closer than that between astronomy and Scripture, we are speaking only of a remote preparation. Should we not be placing within too vague a concept all sorts of different speculations rather as Noe packed into the Ark all the innumerable varieties of created animals? Indirectly any philosophical thesis might be profitable for conversion or for spiritual edification; any monstrosity is capable of good sense in pure and expert hands. But should we make any progress along this line? Would Christian philosophy obtain any consistency as a philosophy?

Certainly the Alexandrians thought so, and Pascal too when he announced: "Plato to incline a man towards Christianity." But they were making a choice; they were limiting the propaedeutic to determined exercises of a metaphysical and moral kind. And at that point the difficulties begin; we have to produce a canon of good thoughts about God. It is the philosopher's task to discover them; but it is the Christian's right to pass judgement on them. In fine, isn't Christian philosophy just a selection of conclusions for the use of the right people, a philosophy which has received blessings and passports from theology? I do not deny that the notion, thus understood, has a certain reality or historical stability, but it seems too clerical to make philosophers quite comfortable; they will feel that they have become little boys again, gathered together to receive prizes, if not a rain of impositions.

It is easy to picture their reactions. If they are well-disposed (which is not always the case), they will respect the traditional labels, and they will perhaps preserve the propaedeutic, but they will ruin its spirit. The revelation which, as philosophers, they will have to put up with will confine itself to re-editing natural philosophy and crowning automatically a rational undertaking which is supposed to have reached its completion. Philosophy will be Christian because it will have appropriated what it considers suitable for Christianizing, casting the rest into the outer darkness, so that in the end one might ask whether the rôles have not been reversed: is reason heralding religion or is religion reaching its completion in the work of reason? From Leibniz to Hegel there are plenty of examples of this putting the cart before the horse, brought about under the patronage of a so-called Christian philosophy. It seems at this point that we are led inevitably to choose between two extreme courses, either an absolute naturalization of Christianity which will dissolve it into the history of philosophy, or an implicit supernaturalization of the philosophical Logos which would oblige us to consider our lightest thoughts as God's supernatural gifts.

But there are, no doubt, between these extremes, more satisfactory interpretations, and I am far from supposing that one cannot make something definite and precise of the idea of a propaedeutic to the Gospel. The point is that each view has a tendency of its own, and, in the present case, the tendency is to suppress the difference in kind between a movement of thought which increases in profundity and a revelation which comes down from God to men. The idea is that humanity should pass by insensible stages from autonomous reflection to obedient faith. A gradual process of this kind is not without its difficulties for a theology and a philosophy which will remain faithful to their respective vocations.

2. A second version of the formula is: *A Christian philosophy is one which undergoes Christian influence, and, as a result, owes its formation to Christianity.* As before, the thesis can take various forms. It may be a question in the first place of direct help given by faith as Laberthonnière and, up to a point, Malebranche considered. Reason would receive

the aid of grace from within; philosophical reflection would be conducted with the categories of revelation themselves. It would not only gain possession of fresh objects which would enlarge its field of vision, but it would be nourished by a heavenly manna and derive from this its principles, its method and its soul.

How could a philosophy thus specifically Christian and intrinsically supernatural fail to be confused with theology pure and simple? Only by verbal subtleties and arbitrarily constructed lines of demarcation. So most thinkers who believe in an intrinsic influence of revelation on philosophy mean by it something which works in an indirect or partial fashion. It is rather a philosophical burgeoning which develops on the basis of revealed data, like ivy on an oak tree; or again, as we have seen in the Augustinian tradition of St Anselm, it is an effort by which thought tries to fill the gaps in the revealed message at the risks and perils of anyone who chooses to set out on such an adventure; or finally it is a sort of extension of the intelligence which relates the message to what it already knows of man and the world, stretching out to it from our side and thus forming a field of inquiry half-way between what we ourselves discover and what we receive.

Fr Gratry states the necessity of this illumination from on high quite boldly: "I rely only on grace", he said, "to bring reason within the limits of reason." But if we scrutinize this declaration we find that a no-man's-land is excluded. There are only two domains and they are in no way confused. Christianity becomes the guiding star of speculation. The latter is considered quite impotent if it is left to its own resources, but it is only sick. Gratry does not kill it; he recognizes its autonomy.

Still less pessimistic than Gratry and, *a priori*, than the traditionalists, Etienne Gilson is nevertheless in this tradition. He considers that philosophy is Christian in so far as it is made possible by Christianity, supported by it and engendered by it. He does not believe that this assistance is purely external and objective, since it is more or less inevitably experienced by the believing soul. So he considers philosophy to be Christian if it "accepts the regulative action of Christian dogma". To explain how an extra-rational source influences reason, he is content to declare: "Faith proposes solutions, and then philosophy sometimes succeeds in finding demonstrations."[1] On the whole this is certainly the most satisfactory way of presenting the view which we are considering, but the author leaves us unsatisfied.

3. In the third place one may understand *philosophy to be Christian when it inherits from Christianity*. This view differs from the preceding one in that it is compatible with the disappearance, whether real or imagined, of faith. St Anselm, again, has shown us the birth of this idea: even if I lose the faith, he said, I should not be able to renounce that knowledge of the divine being which faith has enabled me to acquire. In commenting on this, I used the image of a residual magnetism.

On a less limpid and less innocent interpretation of this view one could, so to speak, decant Christianity into a *gnosis* and allow philosophical speculation to take it over altogether. Jacob Boehme and Hegel have attempted this. Mystery, for them, is no longer supernatural, or at least they are so much at ease with it that it has become something quite within their rational capacity. Their philosophy is coextensive with the secrets of the Most High and is his sole legatee.

Let us now suppose that we are regarding Christianity from outside as a historical fact foreign to our own convictions. We could still take an interest in it and gather up fragments of it for general use according to our own way of thinking. This would not be a Christian philosophy constructed by Christians for Christians, but all the same it would be a

---

[1] *La Philosophie chrétienne* (Le Saulchoir, Juvisy), pp. 64–70.

philosophy of Christianity, originated or occasioned by the
existence of Christians. It would be hypothetico-deductive[2];
just as a mathematician can deduce all the consequences of a
postulate, we could discover all the implications of a revealed
principle and leave the truth of our conclusions dependent
upon the original condition, which itself remains beyond the
scope of our judgement. Modern thought would offer more
than one example of such a process: for example, Kant's
a priori can serve to bring together a whole chain of representations and give them a structure without having itself any
ontological value. Nearer to our own time, Husserl puts in
inverted commas the metaphysical reality of this or that
essence which he has been led, nevertheless, to describe and
to analyse in great detail. On these models and on such
foundations many different philosophies of Christianity might
be constructed.

But we have not yet completed the tale of the possible
meanings of a Christian inheritance. Often it refers to the
decay of the message in a profane civilization which laicizes
it, swallows it up and eventually travesties its terms. It is a
law of history that faith tends to grow cold as it spreads over
a larger area; it is menaced both by the ideologies into which
it enters and by those which it brings into being; if the source
was religious, the results hardly deserve that name. Philosophy
often undertakes tasks of demolition; it achieves with its
eyes open what the passage of time would have accomplished
less consciously and more slowly. And the old stones are used
for building a new house. The fragments are Christian, but
the synthesis is not. So Voltaire and Rousseau evacuate the
specific dogmas of Christianity and retain only a philan-
thropical aroma. The eighteenth century tried to kill faith in
the Incarnation in favour of a humanitarian morality. Far
more radical still than this blood-transfusion and this change

---

[2] That is, it would be a deduction founded upon a hypothesis, not
upon an evident principle.

of level is the Marxist movement. This acknowledges its Christian antecedents and has a certain affection for them as past events. But after giving a place in history to each of its predecessors, dialectical materialism excludes them all from the absolute, in which it establishes itself and only itself.

4. The fourth possible formula is the following: *a Christian philosophy is one which relates itself to Christianity as to an order which is different from it and superior to it*. In its vaguest manifestations, it consists at least in an avowal of insufficiency. This is the attitude of all pious agnosticisms. Their critical meditation ends honestly in a homage to an absolute which is beyond their grasp. If philosophy is the act of doubting, it must allow that it cannot attain to ultimate reality and it will logically content itself with a subordinate place. It must hold itself ready to give way to sources of certitude other than pure reflection if such exist.

Furthermore it can then become for the believer a redoubtable weapon against unbelief. Starting with Ecclesiastes we can see how great is the power of attack deployed by the dialectic of reduction: it devastates anti-religious dogmatisms and leaves nothing standing but the One. For this dangerous weapon cannot be used against those who have first employed it: it calls the One that which resists the acid of rationalism, and it proclaims from the housetops that this residuum is the object of faith or of an intuition which escapes reason's clutches. The divine "super-essence" of Pseudo-Dionysius thus profits from the destructive work of Sextus Empiricus. The mystical dialectician who puts explosives in the enemy's citadel sometimes has no need to give himself so much trouble; it is enough for him to show up the contradictions in which his adversaries are involved, and their positions blow up at once of their own accord before the apologist's eyes.

However, the method of reduction is not tied to this particular technique, and in the hands of believers who are also philosophers it can give rise to fine developments of thought.

Although it has recourse to reason in order to limit reason's pretensions, it does not content itself with keeping all finite beings away from the absolute, but it also emphasizes the imperfections of such beings so as to throw clearer light on the affirmation of God and its inviolable character or to demand reason's respect for God's revelation. This positive rôle of the philosophers of insufficiency derives, on the whole, from Kant and his disciples, since they support knowledge in order to leave room for a belief which critical thought cannot disallow. In spite of the master's own reserves about Christianity, he provided Protestant, and sometimes also Catholic, apologetics with some noteworthy ideas during the nineteenth century; he has given a Christian colouring to the philosophies not only of Fichte and Ritschl but also of T. H. Green and Boutroux, to quote a few names almost at random.

Still more interesting is the reintegration of myth into metaphysics. The repercussions of this upon our problem are obvious enough. It was recognized in antiquity that philosophy comes up against certain limits, and that to avoid meaningless or misleading ratiocination it is proper to use symbolic descriptions or stories, since we cannot subject a transcendent reality to a rigorous analysis. This was Plato's view, and his work offers us a whole range of procedures to supplement pure thought, from the allegory of the cave, which is an illustration, to the myth of Er the Armenian, which is a dream, by way of Atlantis, which is perhaps partly a memory. The sense of the divine mystery, which is so deeply embedded in the Christian consciousness, was to act in the same way, all the more so because Christianity gives to historical events and to saintly individuals a quite new importance; ideas are not everything—they are dependent on a reality which surpasses them and which they invoke but cannot designate.

If we may believe Paul Ricœur, St Augustine made use of a "mythical" philosophy for reasons which were still more precise; for, in virtue of a need for unity which neo-Platonism had already impressed upon him, he thought it impious to multiply principles: to admit two principles, one good and the other bad, would be absurd and blasphemous. There was thus no need to seek a philosophical explanation of evil, which would be an undertaking doomed to failure and indeed reprehensible; instead one must return to "myth", that is, to the fall of Adam and Eve of which the Bible tells us. It does not seem to me that this interesting interpretation is imposed upon us by the facts in the case of St Augustine, for he passed from Manicheism to neo-Platonism by a different route: he suddenly realized that all beings were good in so far as beings; evil was always an aspect or a phase of a being, not a substance in itself. And this discovery, which freed the young rhetorician from a metaphysical anguish, remained with him in spite of his later pessimism about the sinful will and its inability to substitute for grace. The creature, as it comes from the hand of God, is fundamentally good; the interplay of the self and its faculties which makes us what we are is a gift of God and a joyful effervescence of being, whereas evil is a privation and ontologically secondary. This last thesis is not, in St Augustine, the occasion for those convenient sophistries which were sometimes produced by the apologists who followed him. But, whatever may have been the Saint's intellectual history, the result is clear: he does not attempt to resolve the problem of evil in conceptual terms, but thinks it wiser to have recourse, for the appeasement of the mind, to the book of Genesis. The account of the Fall corresponds with a philosophical modesty faced by an order of things which cannot be adequately penetrated. On the basis of this example we can therefore give a place within philosophy to certain revealed data which for the philosopher are not strictly explanations but approximate, yet most valuable, representations.

Another contemporary writer, G. Gusdorf, attributes to

myths a permanent function in metaphysics. Instead of under-standing them as mythological accounts of a suspect and degraded kind, we must look for their fundamental teaching; it has for its purpose to put us in touch with reality, to picture for us the various types of existence and their signi-ficance, and to regain the concreteness of actual living which reason has abandoned. "Giving the world of man a meaning", that is the service which myth performs, and if criticism must purify it genuine knowledge must not repudiate it, for no metaphysic can repudiate the task of integrating us with the whole. Logical necessity is a rule of the game for intel-lectual analysis. But the unity which is man carries with it the need for another sort of movement, "an active prejudice of the thinker" which accepts the meaning of human destiny and the values which relate to it. Myth thus expresses not an inertia but an awareness of total solidarity and of what is most fully determinate. This cannot be got rid of with-out bringing it in again by the back door. It reveals and helps to make intelligible the structure of existence. This is certainly true of the Christian mysteries, which are an un-failing source of explanations, and Gusdorf quotes J. Rivière's very illuminating remark: "They explain not because they summarize reality, but because they are themselves part of the reality which has not lent itself to summarization." Mysteries, being inexplicable, are not directly proved. But they prove themselves by what they explain. They are the pledges of the eternal in space and time. In a certain sense, then, there is nothing superior to philosophical myth and that is just what makes it indispensable: it offers reason the unity which evades it and without which it loses its own meaning.

Ricœur and Gusdorf do suggest to us that Christian philo-sophy shows the insufficiency of philosophy. Should we not go further and say, with Maurice Blondel, that it is first and foremost a philosophy of insufficiency, not because it is itself lacking in anything but because it marks out the territory

in which Revelation operates? Thus the Christian philosopher's story is that of a man who first reacts against the
idea of Christianity which arises spontaneously in his mind,
seeks the means of escaping from it and is led eventually by
the failure of his attempts to postulate the solution which he
wished to avoid.[3] This struggle with himself is the guarantee
of rational autonomy. The "myth" is no longer a mere background for the thinker's mind nor is it a hard indigestible
lump. It is no longer even a force which compensates for
reason's deficiencies, as these writers whom we were quoting
just now would have it; it is bound up with reason, yet it
does not originate in reason; it transforms reason by requiring
acceptance by reason and by respecting reason's free disposal
of itself. Reason eventually proclaims that it is necessary,
but that it is not possible for our nature to engender it. In
virtue of the grace which transcends it, reason marks out the
object which will accomplish its innermost desire, and this
desire itself would remain unknown to it if it had not encoun-
tered the transcendence of the supernatural. Thus it knows
itself in its innermost citadel through that which is the wholly
Other.

On the nature of such a bond between philosophy and grace,
which gives the maximum autonomy to the former and the
maximum transcendence to the latter, disquisitions deriving
from Blondel are exuberant and sometimes, if I may so put
it, lush. H. Duméry interprets the master's words limpidly,
maintaining that, according to him, the supernatural is postu-
lated necessarily by philosophical reflection which is properly
conducted, but that the necessity is altogether hypothetical
and formal. It is for each one of us to make an act of faith
if he sees fit; but this is not a matter for which philosophy
itself takes responsibility. "The supernatural is for the philosopher a necessary hypothesis; only theology can bear upon
its reality. Blondel, as a philosopher, does not require that

[3] H. Duméry, *Blondel et la religion* (Paris, 1954), p. 65.

the supernatural should exist; he requires that it should be possible. It is the hypothesis of the supernatural, not its reality in actual fact, which conditions the validity of natural ontology."[4] So, then, a philosophy which is true to its whole vocation cannot dispense itself from raising the religious problem; and, having done so, it cannot exclude the supernatural perspective or regard this as optional. It owes it to itself to make us give faith a trial; it cannot give it to us or substitute itself for our own will, however far it presses on with its investigations and its theoretical presentiments.

This distinction effected at the last moment between the order of reflection or essence and that of faith or existence saves Blondelianism from the charge of reducing revelation to a mere extension or development of nature. But isn't this done at the cost of a very abrupt demarcation between philosophy and life, as if philosophy were only a logic relative to presuppositions or conclusions whose reality it cannot judge but only their intelligible connections?

Blondelianism proves not to be without its difficulties. But one thing, at any rate, is clear: apart from Blondelianism and the interpretation of it given by Duméry, it would be a vain hope to look for any watertight meaning of the expression "Christian philosophy". The conceptions of Christian philosophy which we have examined above are in fact for the most part forms of theology; or, more precisely, they rely on the presence of faith, even if their content does not refer directly to it, for they represent the judgement which a Christian can pass on certain types of philosophy, looking at them from outside, or which the historian makes, in a general way, about certain parts of the history of philosophy which flourish in a Christian atmosphere. Thus the adjective *Christian* could not be applied by the philosopher himself to the philosophy as such. In this respect the epithet would be extrinsic, like light

[4] *Op. cit.*, p. 118.

falling upon an object. Blondel, on the other hand, undertakes to construct a religious philosophy which can claim such a qualification at least in some vague way without thereby incurring the reproach of overlooking the barrier which philosophers and theologians alike imperatively demand between their two disciplines, a barrier overlooked perhaps by Laberthonnière, who was so close to Blondel in his early days but was destined to part company with him in the end. Blondel's attempt is thus extremely attractive and also difficult. It does not fully convince, but it does attract one, and it is the best approximation to the truth which we at present have.

Its weak point concerns the philosophical necessity of the supernatural. Duméry seeks to establish, in regard to this, a subtle equilibrium, but he cannot win everybody's vote for it. Other interpreters require either more necessity or less. In the first case, Christianity remains, but philosophy withers; in the second, philosophy remains but Christianity moves into the background. In either case Christian philosophy is compromised: the noun absorbs the adjective or *vice versa*. This is particularly the case if one falls back upon a vague idea of the insufficiency proclaimed by the philosopher. A reflection which is closed in upon itself may well be incompatible with the mind's movement towards faith, but is it sufficient that reflection should be open to outside influence for it to be called specifically Christian? The axioms and the requirements engendered in us by revelation will not really show themselves, after all, until after our acceptance of revelation and might well have provoked nothing at all remarkable in the original exercise of our reason, however well-disposed that may have been. It is obvious that the needle has to move only a little way to the left or the right, and Christian philosophy will become either impossible in the one case or indispensable in the other.

What emerges from these discussions is that the direction of thought indicated by Blondel must be adopted but on condition that it is revised and taken further. It breaks at once with an inhuman and out-of-date notion of philosophy according to which we should be able here below to discover straightway the last word about the natural and supernatural orders, to put the whole of reality into a conceptual form which is always adequate, and to make closed and complete systems, whereas in fact we can do no more without fear of error than determine certain directions and take certain soundings. Christian philosophy has no hope of finding a home in any such rigid and systematic classification; thus it would make sense only *per denominationem extrinsecam*, as a general compatibility of philosophy with theology. But there are not many Christians so simple-minded as to believe that the task of philosophy on this earth is as easy as all that and to confuse the knowledge of this life with the vision of the next. Blondel realizes this; he offers us a speculation which is based, let us repeat, on the critical awareness of our insufficiency and on the duty of leaving nothing undone to discover on what conditions it can be remedied.

Moreover he does not allow the philosopher to overlook his true condition, that is, in the end, the supreme options which control his destiny as they pass through the prism of his reflection. It may be the case that Blondel gave a Christian orientation to this because he was a Christian himself. But it does not follow that he has not thus revealed philosophy's innermost soul or at any rate its most urgent problem. He has helped it to formulate what it has sought, gropingly and in substance, for two thousand years and perhaps for its whole history: not only a judgement upon its power and its limits, but a rational expectation of the word which would be spoken from heaven if heaven should speak. The absolute thus grafted upon human thought is present to it only in a tragic and prospective sense; it works upon it through a sort of fruitful absence. What we chiefly owe to the Blondelian doctrine of insufficiency is our deliverance from the easy-going air and the complacent psittacism which have so often tarnished the renown of Christian philosophy. Far from being a soft option, it is a state of tension: the adjective and the noun do not make an altogether peaceful pair; they clash in spite of their attraction for one another, and they involve a paradox, for they are both heterogeneous and indissoluble at the same time. And it is perhaps by this painful and laborious route that the philosophies will one day achieve their unity. They all know well enough that they are in pursuit of it, and each of them must admit the truth of this in its own case unless it has an obstinate attachment to a system and a special gift of blissful ignorance about its own wretched state. Why, then, should not a thinker offer us a promise which is at the same time a programme and, if he sets himself to the task, attempt the great adventure of proclaiming by his thought the conditions for the fulfilment of thought, even if the liberation for which we hope joins with an initiative from above and profits by it? The philosopher, subject to the common fate of gaining truth only little by little and with the sweat of his brow, perceives in this condition the only sort of sufficiency which can come to him. And then he is beginning to face the issue.

PART III

TOWARDS A SYNTHESIS

"A man is a philosopher", an expositor of Plotinus wrote recently, "when he forms for himself methodically a vision of the world, but above all when he questions his implicit presuppositions, when he unceasingly criticizes his own system and the movement of his thought so as to benefit from them all the more in the long run."[1] Altering this definition very slightly, I should like to say that the philosopher is a man who undertakes to marshal *all* his resources so that he may attain the truth; unlike the scholar, he is not content with a partial mobilization, still less with a merely random employment of his powers. It is almost inevitable that such an attitude should make the philosopher a metaphysician; for the mind, by questioning itself without restriction, soon comes to pass a judgement on the universe without restriction and seeks to determine its nature absolutely; metaphysics, if it is possible, has as its ambition to discover the origin and the destiny of beings by a critical examination of the phenomena manifested by them. To put it shortly, let us conclude that philosophy and metaphysics aim at constituting, in accordance with the requirements of an absolute honesty and an unrestricted reflection, the universal kingdom of true affirmations.

This reference to certain elementary definitions of philo-

---

[1] J. Trouillard, *La Purification plotinienne* (Paris, 1956), p. 2.

sophy will lead us to consider our whole problem afresh. Although the preceding chapters have indicated the route which we are to follow, the notion of Christian philosophy is still equivocal. Why do certain writers reject it unless they suppose it incompatible with rational autonomy or because it runs the risk of introducing into objective reflection an extravagant subjectivity or again because it cannot be valid for everybody, for believers and unbelievers? It is sometimes added that philosophy is entirely a matter of demonstrating, and, in these conditions, will not a philosophy which becomes Christian ruin the distinction between nature and grace which believers and unbelievers have a common interest in maintaining? Such are the objections which we have now to examine, and they are closely connected with generally accepted principles which are implied by our definitions.

When we considered Christian philosophy to be a "dramatic" reflection, we were using rather questionable language. Such an approach immediately encounters obstacles, and it can win no acceptance unless it can turn them into springboards. For Christianity will have no value for philosophy unless it can provoke the thinker to open up new routes instead of dispensing himself from thought. This sort of reflection must be a way of cooperating with the progress of philosophy. And we know that progress in this field is equivalent as a rule to the conquest of a region which had been previously considered non-philosophical. All philosophy has a "beyond" which it would, if possible, delimit and reduce. This hazard will be surmounted, or surmountable, if we can show that Christian philosophy is not a hybrid and inconsistent product, but a way of purifying philosophy itself. On what conditions, if any, can it give precision to the critical autonomy, the objectivity and the universality of pure philosophy? Will it give us a better understanding of the difference between nature and grace? Philosophy and Christianity are each a sort of purgatory for the other; it would be a great thing to reach the conclusion that Christian philosophy can pass within its own sphere through the purgatory which is first proposed to it from outside, to prove or to glimpse the truth that the most complete philosophy is in this sense the philosophy which is *also* Christian, while the most complete Christianity is that which is *also* a philosophy.

CHAPTER VII

THE CHRISTIANIZING OF PHILOSOPHY AND CRITICAL AUTONOMY

Henri Gouhier considers that philosophies are of two kinds. Some, which he calls philosophies of *truth*, start from the real and try to explain it or to account for it in virtue of principles which are, by hypothesis, outside or above the real. The others, which he calls philosophies of *reality*, make it their one aim to put us in touch with the concrete; they suppose that principles can be perceived, but the difficulty is to have the mind's eye purified enough to catch sight of them. Is it possible, then, for a Christian philosophy to exist? Everything depends on the type of thought which we shall choose. "A philosophy of truth does not seem to us capable, as such, of being a Christian philosophy; but in so far as the philosopher is wedded to the possession and the description of the real, the shadow of the Christian believer is cast upon this world as he comes to see it, and this he would offer to all intelligent creatures. A Christian philosophy is thus a philosophy Christianized by the presence of a reality, which is man's history in his relations with God."[1]

[1] H. Gouhier, *La Philosophie et son histoire* (Paris, 1944), p. 44.

M. Gouhier is contrasting, in fine, the spirit of criticism and the spirit of acceptance. In practice, he acknowledges, they are found together: it is a question of dominant characteristics, not of exclusive categories. It is apparently only a truism to say that the philosophies in the first category cannot be described as Christian, and we are back in the enclosure where all the adversaries of Christian philosophy, whatever their particular colour, always take refuge. They conceive of philosophy, first and foremost, as a customs-house officer charged with sorting out the importations of our knowledge and allowing them free passage only if they first satisfy the existing rules and the criteria of coherence. Every thinker worthy of his calling has, therefore, to scrutinize the pretensions of empirical knowledge; he must have the art of putting all in doubt, a tendency to reject and to economize. To philosophize is to be prepared, out of a love of truth, to take a strong line with any authority whatsoever until the necessary verifications are forthcoming; in the end philosophy becomes identified with a fearless logic; it is simply the application of this to the whole field of inquiry. In this checking and controlling movement which defines it, it immediately shuns everything which is not its own law. It leaves religious beliefs on one side, and has nothing to do with Christian influences. *Ex hypothesi*, it cuts off everything except the cold, immanent light of the judgement.

That is what it looks like at first sight. But I wonder whether appearances are not deceptive. M. Gouhier would admit, I think, that philosophy is not entirely a matter of criticism and that it must also make positive proposals. And there is more to it than this. Even in its critical function, supposing that we could isolate it, it remains strangely suggestible, subject to mysterious influences. Can we seriously suppose that philosophy can be reduced to dodging contradictions? The necessity of our reasoning must depend on causes which are less purely formal. Our starting-points or initial postulates would have to be justified, which is strictly impossible, yet would be of capital importance. And then, can a philosophy claim to need no fresh sources of supply in the course of its development? One must refuel during a long voyage. Philosophers do this as naturally as they breathe, sometimes without noticing it. Again can one be so sure of finding the contradictory of a given proposition? Some centuries ago one might have thought so: but it has become rash to maintain it in the present state of mathematical analysis and of logistics, which show us what madness it would be to empty out the shades of meaning involved even in our everyday judgements. Our philosophical judgements, in view of their density, would require an eternity in which to be hammered out correctly into wholly clear propositions. If the evidence which the philosopher uses depended on such a process of simplification and not on the effectiveness of the ideas which he has been sensible enough to adopt, no one would have ever written the first page of a philosophical treatise. Leibniz himself agrees, since he builds his whole system on the principle of sufficient reason as well as on that of non-contradiction.[2]

In point of fact, when the Scholastics sprinkle their demonstrations with principles which they declare *per se evidentia*, when Descartes appeals to clear and distinct ideas and Pascal to the "heart", and when Malebranche at once perceives the superiority of man over the brutes, all of them, to whatever schools of thought they belong, consider that criticism depends upon a certain intellectual *taste*, without which it would be impossible to think correctly, just as it would be impossible to appreciate a painting if one had no aesthetic taste. Reason is a taste for the truth, which implies both the

[2] Need I insist that philosophical salvation does not consist in abandoning the principle of non-contradiction in favour of sentiment, but in basing oneself on a reflection of the widest scope which involves complex techniques?

love of truth and the capacity for it. It possesses a power of discernment which can never be covered by a collection of formal rules. If it could be, it would enter a valley of dry bones and become hopelessly platitudinous.

I am not sure that the implications of all this are always faced. What it amounts to is that the exercise of reason cannot be divorced from the thinker's life. The philosopher is a man; in all his human activities he passes judgements; and in all his judgements he develops, well or ill, his personality as a rational creature. When he philosophizes, he tries to be impartial, but it would be quite unrealistic to suppose that he does not bring with him, at the very heart of his critical endeavour, his religious or non-religious or anti-religious convictions. I am not saying that we can never discriminate, but that the abolition of the man so as to leave only the critic remaining is chimerical and even unthinkable. Critical philosophy can be and must be a Christian philosophy for Christians, just as it cannot fail to be an anti-Christian philosophy for anti-Christians. Let us put aside pretences and boldly admit the facts. What matters is the development of each particular mind in an act of reflection which is inspired by an absolute honesty—that is the only sort of criticism that is of real importance; it is found where an intellectual attitude and a moral virtue come together, and it carries with it, indissolubly, the destiny of philosophy and the destiny of the individual.

Accepting authorities (revealed or otherwise) or undergoing influences, even at the moment of judging, neither validates nor invalidates the judgement itself in any way. Philosophy will not live or die because it is Christian; what counts is the *way in which* it is Christian. The *quality* of its dependence upon Christianity is of much greater importance than the mere fact of it. If my faith leads me to be impartial, why should not all philosophers congratulate me on it? Why should they disallow it and ask me to leave it behind before

I enter the sanctuary of my meditations? We cannot live without belief of some kind, since belief is, for each one of us, what makes us an absolute unity, although that is something which we are always striving after, something which is always in the future. No doubt the temptation of every believer (in a wide sense)—and this applies also to unbelievers —is to dispense himself from the labour of thought. But this is not necessarily a fatal temptation. Many Christians have no vocation to be philosophers and they can give way, innocently enough, to their tendency to avoid reflection; or, more precisely, they are content to have God's Word without trying to understand it or rousing themselves by means of it to discover the why and wherefore of things. When they are philosophers, they run the risk of making use of their Christianity and introducing pseudo-solutions into their philosophy, instead of serving Christianity by their philosophy. But, again, this abuse of belief is not inevitable and is not confined to Christians. They can, on the other hand, find in the divine Word the requirement of a radical impartiality and the source of an unending purification of their ideas. The religion of the Incarnation and of Pentecost seems, more indeed than any other, calculated to produce, in the minds of those who accept its dogmas, a desire for the whole truth and nothing but the truth. If faith is deep and strong, it invades reason as nourishment, not as poison. It demands loyalty to reason out of loyalty to the Father of lights.

We might say the same about autonomy, which is so closely bound up with the spirit of criticism. It is a very widespread error, and one which is nothing short of disastrous in philosophy, to consider autonomy and independence as synonymous. Fernandez defines philosophy most properly as "the sum of knowledge which reason can acquire by its *own* power". But he obviously means "by its *sole* power", and therein lies the disastrous confusion. His commentators fall into it unsuspectingly along with him. In fact the two expressions are not at all synonymous. Absolute independence would imply that there is nothing in the world save the human consciousness, and everyone rightly attacks this solipsism as a monstrous idea. But we must also attack its corollaries, and therefore dissociate independence, which does not exist, from autonomy, which is one of the purposes of existence. I must undertake my responsibilities and, in a sense, take charge of the whole universe. Philosophy, in its critical aspect, is one of the forms of my autonomy, perhaps the only one which enables me to go so far in putting into the framework of my existence that whole universe into the framework of which I am myself naturally inserted. I have to *establish* my own norms, as our use of the phrase indicates. The absolute can be recognized or misconceived by my own free decision. Causes and final ends are subject, so to speak, to my ratification, my hostility or my indifference. Nothing can enhance personal autonomy more than such an arrangement. But, although I am committed to autonomy when I think, I cannot escape from dependence so long as I exist. My existence is brought about by manifold influences. I come into existence as an effect of nature, and I am worked upon at every moment by other thinking beings who have brought me up and taught me, attacked me or loved me. Among the intersubjective causalities, and the most mysterious of them all, is the relation in which the creature stands to its creator, the relation which Christians call grace.

The experience of psychical awakening shows at every level that liberty springs out of a sort of ontological constraint, that there is a metamorphosis of being and a fresh departure which comes about by reason of the very convergence of the causes and of their success. But nobody seems to notice the devastating enigma which lurks in a child's education, in the conversation of two friends or in a man's prayer to God. Is it not surprising and scandalous that the metaphysical analysis of the influence exercised by one mind on another should have been continually neglected in the history of philosophy, that incomparably less attention should have been paid to it than to the relations between thought and matter? The small amount of interest which the problem has received until quite recently may perhaps explain why such simple-minded precepts are so readily accepted, why our inevitable dependence is written off with a stroke of the pen in the name of a supposedly desirable autonomy.

This is the sophism by which the idea of Christian philosophy is to be eliminated. But it can be done only on paper. Philosophers will continue to do their work in accordance with what they are themselves, and no rulings in the matter will make any difference. Nor must we think that revolt indicates in itself a greater autonomy and less dependence, so that the best way to philosophize would be to turn against one's sources of supply and, in the case with which we are concerned, to expel faith in favour of reason. Unfortunately the problem of impartiality is far more complex than this: refusal is still a dependence on the Other, and its dialectic pursues us as inexorably as that of acceptance. As we saw earlier in discussing the spirit of criticism, the fact that one is oneself is less important than the *way in which* one is oneself.

To sum up, critical autonomy is not menaced by the fact that a philosophy is either more or less Christian; Christian philosophy does not find its limits in that direction. On the contrary, there is a *prima facie* agreement between the autonomous reflection demanded by rational thought and the inspiration of a religious doctrine which associates man with the divine liberty. If the latter is the root, the former will be one of its flowers. And if anyone asks whether the root and the flower are of the same texture, we need not hesitate to reply that they are. When philosophical reflection develops in a Christian soul, it is itself intrinsically Christian; and this includes an ascesis of the mind which dissects, discriminates, advances little by little and is in touch with the corresponding demands which can arise in non-Christian souls. There should be nothing surprising or inhibiting for the Christian about this coincidence in one and the same *Logos*, for he would be lacking in his own faithfulness to it if he failed to recognize it wherever he finds a passion for the truth.[3]

[3] Just as in biology an eye can develop in different species from different embryonic tissues, so philosophy can have origins which are to some extent dissimilar in different individuals, while preserving a constant function and a constant structure. In virtue of its origin it will be Christian in the minds of certain people. In virtue of its function and its structure it will remain in principle a homogeneous category for all minds without distinction.

CHAPTER VIII

THE PROBLEM OF GOD'S SUMMONS

During the period when rationalism reigned triumphant it would have been hopeless to claim even a modest place for faith in philosophy. The situation has greatly changed, and today we speak of philosophical faith readily enough. It refers in the first place to the element of belief without which there is no means of even beginning a process of reasoning, much less of completing one. No system is watertight, however great the genius of its maker, and the most faithful partisan of reason knows that there comes a time when he must believe in its empire without actually beholding it. The existentialists, going further, will require from faith a certitude which pure intellection is too weak to give them: it is not possible to explain all the real—we must understand that it surrounds and transcends us. Gabriel Marcel has said some profound things on the subject, making the distinction between a problem and a mystery. The faith of which he treats in this first sense of the word is a decision which goes beyond explanations and which therefore leads us to make certain judgements with confidence. For a philosopher the most noteworthy article of this faith is perhaps that there is a unity among philosophies, for we never enter a promised land which leaves no mysteries to be explored: we are content to have glimpses of it. The first sense of faith in philosophy, then, is an affirming without an experimental or even intellectual certitude which entirely answers our question. We have had occasion to notice this already and we shall not dwell on it, although it can be understood in two different ways: either as a leap into the irrational or as a reasonable risk, according as there are no guarantees at all or indirect ones.

In the second sense of the expression philosophical faith is not simply the acknowledgement of mystery. It is a generosity by which we agree to commit ourselves for our beliefs. The term "engagement" has been very popular for several years; nor is this surprising, for its success is parallel with that of faith in philosophy; it expresses this in the concrete, and we shall not insist further upon the relevance which Christianity may regain thereby. Rightly or wrongly, our contemporaries are more interested in a practical wisdom than in the niceties of an abstract discussion. Does a philosophy which becomes Christian lose a certain subtlety? It is possible, but the fault, if it is a fault, is not due to its Christianization: rather it shows the characteristic of a period, a practical orientation which is opposed to the gnostic itch of other periods.

There is a third sense in which faith can intervene in philosophy: as an assent to a personal witness. This is a much more surprising sort of intrusion than the previous ones. It seems to bring philosophy down to the level of conversational exchanges or historical conjectures, unless the value of dialogue or the assessment of historical events can be raised to the level of philosophy. This last hypothesis would never have been accepted by Aristotle, who regularly opposes knowledge of generalities to empirical opinion, with which "historical" knowledge is, in his vocabulary, synonymous. Its object is the particular, "becoming" or the accidental. "There can be", he writes, "no systematic study of accidental being, as is clear from the fact that no science, practical, productive or speculative, attempts to treat of it. A man who builds a house does not produce the attributes which accompany the construction, for they are innumerable."[1] But other Greeks did inaugurate a science of this kind, in regard to testimony. Historians, for example, made judicious remarks about the rules for the accuracy of a historical narrative; they advise the writer to choose a subject which forms a natural whole and which is accessible to the observation of the narrator in time and space. Polybius and Thucydides select and arrange their facts so as to seize upon their objective and intelligible connections. They do not doubt the certitude of their art nor its lasting relevance.[2] The theologies of the Christian era have taken it up and have elaborated for apologetic purposes a technique of proofs for Revelation; to them we owe the important idea of a convergence of arguments. In the eighteenth century W. Paley and his colleagues combine these considerations with a curious employment of judiciary procedure and of the scientific calculation of probabilities; the use Newman made of these attempts in his *Grammar of Assent* to outline a psychology of intersubjective certitude is well known. Yet neither historians nor theologians have succeeded in their undertaking, from the philosopher's point of view.

To do this, it would have been necessary for them to face squarely the problem of *summons*. A recent attempt has been made in a fine book, *L'Essence du prophétisme*. "The life of God", we read, "in its Biblical acceptation must not be moralized or rationalized." God appears to man "in the polarity of his pathos, his love and his anger, in his severity and in his mercy. . . . He is not the God of universal principles, but the God of the unique, of the historical moment." The spirit (*ruah*) of God is a vital emotion: an anthropopathic conception, perhaps, but it would be better to call it anthro-

---

[1] *Met.*, E, ch. II.
[2] See texts collected by A. J. Toynbee, *Greek Historical Thought* (New York, 1952).

potrophic (*God turns towards man*). The prophet participates in this divine movement towards man; furthermore, he is summoned by the word (*davar*) of God, he must transmit it, and he must answer it. The whole structure of the Biblical universe is determined by this. "The *ruah* introduced into the world a living God who nevertheless did not modify it. The *word* of God made the universe historical. The universe, now engaged in a dialogue, has a history. By the *ruah*, there was a presence of God in the world. By the *davar* God cooperates with man—God and man meet in an alliance."[1] Knowledge is thus a struggle, a violent explosion. Like the mystical relationship, it can be compared with married love, but it differs from this by the unpredictable suddenness with which it makes its irruption and breaks to pieces the soul of the prophet.

But can this summons enter as such into philosophy? I think not. If it is Greek to reject this extreme, then I am Greek. Christian philosophy does seem to me to draw the line at this point. The thinker's autonomy does not prevent Christianity from entering our thoughts; but the existential intimacy of God's summons does provide an obstacle. The philosopher does not name persons. For him they are a bottomless abyss. It is other people's business to designate them. The historian and the theologian may know Jesus in his earthly life, but the philosopher knows only the ideas which radiate from him. Perhaps there is no philosophy without a standing away from the subject of inquiry. Even the Cartesian revolution, with its introduction of the *cogito* into metaphysics, could only do it by defining the self; what interests Descartes is his thinking substance, not his pure subjectivity apart from all splitting up into subject and object and all reflective putting together again. Still less shall we find a sheer encounter with the other in philosophy, nor any particular dialogue which can be accepted as it stands. All reflection must objectify its subjects in some sort. It moves

[1] A. Neher, *L'Essence du prophétisme* (Paris, 1955), pp. 95–115.

them about and considers them like an artist planning a work; they are properties which tend to exist in themselves without ever really managing to do so.

Between knowledge of a Platonist type which has general ideas as its object and Judaeo-Christian knowledge which resolves itself into living consciousness, there is in fact a form of objectivity which concerns the philosopher and which deserves the fullest study: I refer to the organisms of ideas in which personalities are expressed, elements of an intelligible communion and an ideal reconstruction which can be indefinitely renewed. Thus the Incarnation is, in the mind of the philosopher, an original constellation of concepts, although its source, which is the living Christ, escapes him. Each person is surrounded by a circle of principles which both reveal and conceal him at the same time; he thus fills with his presence the vacuum which separates him from other persons. What he sends forth in this way is not merely a doctrine which he invents or transmits; it is also, and above all, as we find in the case of any genius, the very nature of the man which is mysteriously spread abroad in seeds of thought and which, far from being enfeebled in the process, seem to become ever stronger. Since we have taken the example of Christ, let us say that it is not for the philosopher to invoke him in his ineffable individuality, but that it is proper for him to meditate not only on the wisdom of his words but on the tenor of his life as it has spread throughout the cosmos. In this sense Bethlehem and Golgotha are rational emanations, and every event can become universalized in an anonymous idea Representation, which to a certain extent covers up origins, diffuses presences.

Philosophy is the prism in which the intelligibility of life can be discerned. Like most prisms, it both expresses and transforms the rays of light which pass through it. Christian philosophy cannot pierce through to Christ himself without being brought to a halt; the picture of Christ which it would draw would be vague and inaccurate. The reason for this, as we have just seen, is not that Christ is too high for philosophy to approach, for the latter's bent is to prove everything without hesitation and it is perhaps unaware that mysteries are pointed out in other ways. It is brought to a halt because it cannot escape from its own presuppositions, which commit it to the handling of ideas rather than to direct commerce with persons. I do not maintain that its incapacity arises from the general character of the ideas, for such language is equivocal and would require much clarification. The incapacity of philosophy results rather from the distance at which it stands from persons, from the relative impersonality of its perspectives and its purposes. Philosophy's limitation is its constant preoccupation with such truths as may refashion a whole world; it is the necessity of expounding things to a third party, that is to say the renunciation of direct summons in order to establish indirect communications of all kinds in all directions. Objectivity is a very special kind of inter-subjective relation, which involves impoverishments and sacrifices, but which makes it possible to make contact with the whole world without approaching individuals one by one; it substitutes, as it were, a halting *tutti* for a well-sustained *duo*.

But the mediation of essences, the cold justice of the idea, by no means ties the thinker's hands. He knows well enough how men meet one another, and how they meet God. And by methods of convergence and by the intelligible organisms which it produces in the vacuum between human minds, philosophy disposes those minds not to turn away from particularity as though concrete existence were valueless, whereas in fact it is the justification of all value. Philosophy would not be worth an hour's trouble if it did not prepare for summons. Let us not forget that it also corrects summons, by continuously purifying dialogue from its complacency and its selfish partialities. For, at the fine point of human consciousness, is it the resounding word or the silence which is fully significant? Alternating silences between speakers mark the last stage before that perfect continuity and perfect communion which reveal to each his definitive individuality.

CHAPTER IX

CAN A CHRISTIAN PHILOSOPHY BE UNIVERSAL?

When it is said that a philosophy should be available for everyone and that a Christian philosophy cannot fulfil this requirement, one is inclined to smile. An impartial judge need only ask the objector under what colours he himself is sailing, since there has never been any school of thought which won everybody's adhesion. I know that this move can be countered by another which is just as easy: truth is a matter of right, and it does not depend on votes; it is based on arguments, not on ballot boxes. If in an age of iron, or of ferro-concrete, there is only a handful of metaphysicians mocked at by the crowd, it is the metaphysicians who are right. I have no intention of insulting the greatness of a man who dares to think alone, if his thinking is to the purpose. But after giving all possible weight to the difference between psychology and logic, a certain uneasiness persists. It is not the guffaws of the crowd that disconcert one, but the secular disagreement of the specialists. They claim universality for their metaphysics, and the ink is not yet dry on their pages when their colleagues tear them up.

An academic distinction between fact and right is not enough to get us out of this awkward situation and save us from scepticism. It would be more useful to inspect the incriminated documents more closely, especially the greatest of them. For the disagreements prove to be less serious when differences of vocabulary have been mastered and if, instead of contrasting disciples, one compares the masters. An assiduous and attentive reading of the greatest philosophers does not leave us with the impression that they are radically incompatible. There are always to be found startling correspondences betwen Plato and Aristotle, St Thomas and Hegel, Descartes and Spinoza; even where they contradict one another, their various resources would make it possible for them to make the necessary adjustments and to join together in a higher synthesis. The more we study them the more we find them complementary of one another. In a choir, there must be dissonances; theirs are of this kind, and they do not at all suggest a wild disorder.

And so we may be able to give, after all, an interpretation of the evidence which is the very reverse of pessimistic. It could be that the differences between philosophers come not from the fact that they are all wrong, but from the fact that they are all right in different ways. Reality is so rich and so vast that the explorer returns filled with awe and wonder, with an experience which is never coincident with that of his neighbour. Much patient comparison of these accounts is necessary if the overlappings are to be detected and a map drawn up of this empire in which each has followed his own path. Mistakes, certainly, may have been made, especially in the form of hasty generalizations or pretensions to hegemony. But the accounts owe a good deal of their variety to the wealth of the subject-matter. Systems do not always succeed one another because they are illusory but because reality is always presenting something new to those who scrutinize it with sufficient care.

The real problem is to find the relationship between metaphysics and the individual person, or, if anyone prefers, between philosophy and character. When one first opens a book, one finds a table of contents and a series of theses presented with a splendid detachment as if they had no connection with the thinker himself. But, when the book is better known, it becomes possible to divine the judgement which the author will pass on this or that problem of which he has as yet said nothing. This sort of prophecy is not just a matter of the logic of ideas; more profoundly, it expresses the thinker's intellectual individuality. We do not take seriously enough St Augustine's statement that each of us has his own reason; St Thomas echoes him by opting for a multiplicity of "active intellects", Descartes by preaching his *cogito*, Newman by making the conduct of inferences part of a person's life-history.

How does the thinking subject affect the metaphysics which he constructs? First by his choice of those aspects of being in which he is interested: there are introverted and extroverted philosophers, lovers of causality, those who plumb the depths of the mind when it is turned to God, and others who do not go beyond creatures. Then there is the colouring which the thinker gives to the whole universe by reason of those ideas which are always emanating from his personal being and which express his life-story in abstract terms: not only does he impose a style and an arrangement upon his ideas, but he translates himself in them and is himself a source of new ideas. This sort of causal activity is revealed to us, for example, in the sacrifice and death of Socrates; other instances are the assembling of monads in the complicated and mirror-like mind of Leibniz, the prerogative of duty in Kant's moral code or Fichte's enthusiasm. What these men themselves were in their intellectual and volitional lives is indissolubly bound up with the philosophical discoveries which are attributed to them. The object of these discoveries is not outside them, but inside them—indeed, it *is* themselves; for there is an objective reality of the subject, there is a "being in oneself" proper to those who are "for themselves".[1] Finally, this objectivity of the subject does not only affect the particularity proper to the subject, but in a sense extends to the whole universe which the mind contemplates; for the relationship of the mind with all things is also something belonging to the mind. And therefore, the personality always modifies to some extent the metaphysic of things in that continued interplay in which being gradually unfolds its virtualities and in which all beings contribute to one another's existence by their reciprocal action.

The upshot may be stated as follows: we may discover different metaphysical *orientations*, but the broad outlines of a science of being remain constant. The list of categories may vary in matters of detail, but since men began to think there has been a certain mental equipment available which is kept in being by their discovery of it. Discussion goes on and will always go on about quality and quantity, causality, finality and so forth. The point is that these things *are* discussed; these concepts, that is to say, are rather schemes; the various aspects are inexhaustibly abundant, and the long procession of schemes is never ended. The destiny of metaphysics is chiefly endangered, not by its congenital incompleteness, but by the narrowmindedness of pedants who suppose that they have said the last word because they repeat the same slogans, instead of using them to make a further advance and to convert fresh experiences into axioms.

These reflections only touch the surface of a difficult problem. But, however sketchy, they are necessary if we are to see more clearly whether and in what sense Christian philosophy can claim universality. Like all philosophies, it makes use of schemes, sometimes of very long standing and commonly received; like all philosophies, it tries to make their content more precise and to make progress in a region

[1] The author here uses the language of existentialism in which a knowing subject is described as being "for himself". (*Trans.*).

which is proper to itself, for it expresses that part of reality which corresponds to the thinking experience of a believer. Thus it becomes clear that we have to distinguish within it different degrees of universality. It cannot communicate its whole essence to the outside observer; it can claim to be understood by him only as a coherent hypothesis or "myth". This sort of universality is already considerable; it enabled Sainte-Beuve to write about Port Royal. A universal adherence to it would presuppose that the principles of Christian philosophy were themselves admitted, and when that point is reached the man who understands it also penetrates to the heart of it and professes it. But this will not happen, probably, in a flash: there will be stages to pass through, and the hypothesis will not turn into a certainty until the evidences have become more and more probable. Will not Christian philosophies have different opinions about these also? They may agree in pursuing an autonomous reflection upon the same religious sources, in discovering an insufficiency in philosophy and in attempting to delineate the contours of this insufficiency, but they will set problems for one another nonetheless. They too will be wedded to their personal approaches, and they must begin by understanding one another if they are to unite in the same adhesion to the same particular theses. Yet they would be bad philosophers if they did not aim at universal validity when they put forward their own theses.

I have tried to show that the lot of religious philosophies is not *a priori* less enviable than that of profane ones. Must we conclude that philosophers, Christian or otherwise, are kings in exile and that, despite their ambitions, they are quite helpless and solitary? Let us not exaggerate the difficulties. The personal stamp which metaphysics must always have has itself metaphysical value, all the more so when the metaphysician is a man of genius and when in his universe all the other perspectives of the universe are outlined. That is why a great philosophical work enjoys at least the universality which belongs to artistic masterpieces: it is half-way between the confidences made by the empirical subject and the almost complete objectivity of mathematics. It forms a sort of organism which has its members and its centre, like a symphony.

But, whereas a symphony contains only operative concepts, a philosophical work attempts rather to articulate the structure of the real; it is the canticle of the whole world, whereas the symphony is only another being added to the world. The beauty of a symphony is not alien to the affirmation of truth: it is an emotion which gives birth to representations; but the type of beauty and the type of truth which are special to philosophy, and in particular to metaphysics, belong to a complete reconstruction of the universe by itself at the instance of the thinker. And since this ideal construction would be nothing less than a faithful reproduction of what exists, its purpose appears in this respect quite different from that of the artist's achievement. The reason which is employed in this task feels itself limited in its resources but unlimited in regard to the promises held out to it. It is both my capacity and yours, and in each case the universe is a private representation. But it is also a continued widening progressive of our representations, a norm which invites them to understand and to accept it, a grace which comes to meet them and which works in all things without being reducible to any of them. Christian philosophy is only a way of experiencing with particular vividness this cascade of certainties: the mysterious unity of being, the initiative with which it beckons us on in diverse ways, and the incompleteness of our sketch-maps of the universe.

CHAPTER X

NATURE AND GRACE

A theologian's life is based on the conviction that philosophy is of the natural order, while faith is related to a supernatural reality, the life of God himself, whose revealed word is its objective manifestation. Of course "nature" here has a theological sense quite different from that in which we speak in philosophy of external nature, or of the instinctive self as opposed to the reason and the will. God *gives* man a nature; and he *gives himself* to this nature in the supernatural, associating it with an intra-divine life which is by definition inaccessible for any creature left to its own resources and is therefore a gratuitous elevation. Such is the tradition of Christian orthodoxy. But how has this duality been represented? To describe a complex situation it has been necessary to use metaphors. An examination of these will be of great value for our inquiry.

1

The first metaphor is that of *stages*: nature is on the ground floor, and the life of grace on the floor above. The latter does not destroy its foundation but tends to correct it and to complete it. "Grace does not abolish nature", says a maxim of the Schools, "but perfects it." The very form of the metaphor suggests a double ontological level and favours the idea of a double end if only in theory; the building could have existed without its upper floor. A higher purpose supervenes upon a more elementary structure.

Some will consider this substructure as imperfect, others as altogether rotten, so that each group will make use of its own metaphors. A Catholic will tend to compare God's action upon us to the playing of an invisible artist upon the two registers of nature and grace, whereas the Protestant will say *simul justificatus, simul peccator*, and will never reconcile Adam with himself in this valley of our exile. But the general scheme of two levels is available for all the Christian confessions. It is implied in the religious philosophies of the Middle Ages and remains in Descartes and Pascal, and in Boyle and Kierkegaard also. It is still presupposed by the notion of Christian philosophy which we have found in E. Gilson.

But there is another picture employed in the Christian tradition, less frequently to be found since the Middle Ages than it was in the time of the Fathers. At the beginning of this century, however, it suddenly assumed a fresh importance, and it tends today to replace the previous metaphor, although the fact is not always consciously recognized. It is a matter no longer of contrasting a basic with an upper stage but of contrasting an *inside* with an *outside*, a source with a derivation, a hidden vocation with a visible expression. The inside is grace; the outside is nature. The believer considers that in his innermost being he is constituted by a divine exigence which appoints him to life in God and for God. But at the same time he is convinced that this exigence requires his historical existence as a man among men. Nature remains for him a previous reality in the sense that it can never reach up to God's supernatural plan for this world; it is radically inadequate and falls short of absolute union with the transcendent reality; but, although this incapacity involves a chronological anteriority, it is also proper to think that nature manifests grace in terms of time and follows after it. It prepares the way for a human response and for a divine effusion because it first obeys a summons which establishes it in its own true being as nature. It is essentially a mediator, always secondary in the order of being and of value, but primary in our conscious awareness and in the course of events. We cannot fix its limits without going beyond them; we cannot exactly determine its own end until we have declared it insufficient. In short, all that nature is must be defined by contrast with grace, yet by means of grace, of which, although it is continually presupposed, it is also the result. The notion of externality applies to it to indicate its character as a derivation, but there is now a general unwillingness to repre-sent transcendence by the picture of a higher level, extending our experience by elevating it. The life of religion (of which philosophy is an aspect) becomes a homage of a centrifugal kind or an expression of our freedom in regard to that source of inspiration which grace is. We prove our faithfulness to God by working to free the world and to fulfil nature's being.[1]

I shall not claim that Blondel has explicitly preferred this way of looking at things to that described previously, but he certainly tends in that direction, and that, no doubt, is why he reproaches Gilson with comparing the data of faith with those of philosophy and effecting a concordance between them, at the risk of compromising both the transcendence of

[1] Parallel with this evolution, a change is taking place in the choice of metaphors to describe revelation. The picture of a *perceptible dialogue* between the Creator and his prophet is much less employed today than that of a *historical line or spiral*, certain points on it reveal-ing the divine initiative and giving a transcendent meaning to the human process, especially in the succession of religious geniuses which culminates in Christ.

faith and the autonomy of philosophy. For Blondel, philosophy reveals the summons of grace in establishing itself in all its determinations as philosophy; and, in this respect, it is not the handmaid of theology, for there is no comparison between the two.

II

A metaphor is not the same as a thought; it is incurably vague or at least incomplete and equivocal. No doubt it would falsify the Christian mentality to confine it altogether to one or other of the outlooks which we have just mentioned. The advantage of the first is that it shows the primacy of faith and its rights over the believer's whole being; the advantage of the second is that it shows the autonomy of philosophical activity. The disadvantage of the first is that it subordinates the basis to the summit to such an extent that, as E. Bréhier would bluntly say, the philosopher's liberty becomes illusory. But the risk run by the second is no less for a Christian, for philosophy, being Christian only in virtue of an inspiration hidden in the depths of the heart and in the end ineffable, undoubtedly gives the impression of identifying itself with a merely profane undertaking. Grace becomes a secret garden, and it promotes philosophy only by inspiring the philosopher with zeal and giving him a more lively nostalgia for infinite perfection which is beyond his reach.

So these pictures, however attractive, must be used with care. And it is therefore with genuine diffidence that I propose a third metaphor: it is that of an *osmosis* or transmutation which, across the centuries and despite the cross-currents of history, enriches nature little by little with the revelation of supernature. St Paul seems to suggest this when he speaks of an engrafting of man into Christ. Certain illustrations of this may be given. It has often been remarked that the initiatives of charity tend to become consolidated as institutions of justice. St Vincent de Paul takes in abandoned children, and thus goes beyond the demands of actual morality; three centuries later the governments of all countries realize that it is their duty to take the place of missing parents. What was once a matter of grace and charity now becomes, if one may so put it, a superior form of nature and justice. The frontiers of nature are thus pushed forward in course of time; nature grows, thanks to supernature. In the same way I should be inclined to believe that our ideas about God are normally destined to develop and to include what was at first beyond the capacities of pure nature. Philosophy, always lagging behind the fine point of the believer's soul, assimilates God's secrets in the course of time through a divine disposal which is always gratuitous in our regard and which, at each fresh stage, awakens in us desires which we had not suspected. We speak without embarrassment about supernatural morality, and in certain cases the expression is a requisite for theology. Why should one not speak of supernatural metaphysics, although the expression is an unfamiliar one? It is legitimate at least in the sense that autonomy benefits from grace and that reason is transformed as the lump is raised by the leaven. No doubt morality is subject to a lawgiver and a judge, whereas metaphysics lays down laws itself and judges without the need of witnesses. But is it not also the acceptance of an absolute which establishes it and instructs it? Is there nothing which is presented to it as its own fulfilment? Who could dare, without fear of self-contradiction, to limit the activity of the Absolute upon our thought and to bid it keep within bounds?

This way of looking at things is to some extent similar to that described by the second of our two metaphors, but it can never involve the "profanation" of a philosophy which bears the name of Christian. Certainly a human person cannot fulfil his destiny without positing and freely constructing a world of his own. But this movement cannot be exclusively centrifugal. All interpersonal influence, and *a fortiori* the dwelling of a divine principle in us, must develop into grateful acknowledgement. A consciousness is no less autonomous because it becomes progressively aware of its causes. The perfection of reason is not ingratitude. Reason is fully adult only in so far as it integrates those organisms of ideas which derive from the divine activity, recognizing it as such. It seems to me that the consummation of reason would be a thanksgiving to God for giving us Christianity. Meditating upon this inexhaustible theme, it would take its stand and proclaim in its own way that Christianity is the finest and truest religion in the world. I have said that philosophy does not embrace a personal summons within its scope, and I still maintain that. That is why philosophy will never be theology or spirituality. It is not its duty, strictly speaking, to issue such a summons, although it can prepare us for it. But there can be a continual interaction between reason and faith: the God of faith leaves the imprint of his countenance upon the God of reason, and reason is thus raised little by little to an acquired knowledge which participates paradoxically but really in the infused or supernatural knowledge of the theologians.

Philosophy is at one and the same time a critical review and an acceptance of a truth with which the mind is invested. When a philosopher receives the supernatural message into his philosophy and distils it in his own fashion as a world-principle, he is embarking upon an enterprise which is both philosophical and Christian, and he must be judged by the power of intelligibility which his affirmations prove to possess. No one can forbid him his attempt *a priori* or take umbrage at the title which he claims. Genius is unpredictable; talent is hard to come by; and Christian philosophy certainly needs both of them to fulfil its destiny. But it is a splendid adventure, for philosophy is attempting in this to be more and more faithful to itself, to enlarge the body of thought which can bind man perpetually to the generosity of God. In the supernatural order, as in the natural, philosophy's mission is to make use of ideas for the development of persons, that is to say, to form the personality in the novitiate of objectivity and renunciation. Perhaps the end of time will manifest more and more the subtle alliance which links together the fecundity of faith and the progress of reason. For if the end and object is the One, it cannot split our minds.

A Chinese friend once told me that when he came to study the West his greatest surprise was to discover the ideas of substance and person, which are both quite foreign to the tradition of the Far East. "The first", he said to me, "comes to you from the Greeks, the second from Christianity." Perhaps this summary account of the matter needs qualification, for the Stoics had a notion of person and Christianity has not left untouched the Hellenic notion of substance. But the remark shows very well to what an extent the human reason, whose fundamental tendencies remain always the same, is subject to moulding processes and accretions in the course of time which we may quite fail to recognize. We have a tendency to forget that we are not at the end of our task, that we have to *become* reasonable and thus to discover little by little the true lineaments of reason itself, these being always less clear in ourselves than they are in pure spirits. . . . That is why an *a priori* refusal to consider the possibility of a Christian development of metaphysics may well be only the result of inertia or of a state of panic induced by the very suggestion of refashioning mental habits.

It is true that the task of outlining the significance, or even the process, of rational development is no easy one. Bréhier once described the history of philosophy as a diastole followed by a systole. At certain periods thought spreads out and becomes diluted in religion, art or politics; then there is a period of critical recollection which saves reason's rights from the dangers which threatened them. The pattern is often true to the facts. Must we not conclude that reason, despite its rigorousness, takes on fresh horizons and undergoes changes to a certain extent as its content changes?

Could one not even speak, in connection with Christian philosophy, of a conversion of reason? It seems clear that one could. However, categories and methods are not turned altogether inside out or upside down by a supernatural polarity; they are made more precise and more penetrating. How could our reason undergo disconcerting changes when it is itself a perpetual demand for intelligible unity? It is not a provisional equilibrium of representations, or merely a taste for synthesis, but a desire to transcend its own limits in order to become true, a disinterested inquiry orientated to the transcendent, so that one may call it an autonomy and an obedience at the same time. It evolves by throwing itself open to values whose consistency seems to it more and more successfully verified, and the capacity to do so is innate in it. When it conceives the notion of a supernature and when it is faced by a message purporting to come to it from above, it is transformed not so much by rejecting its previous principles as by completing them and improving upon them. To repeat, reason realizes that it is human, that is to say, subject to realities which are mysterious and beyond its grasp; and yet it is by realizing this that it is fortified in its universal vocation. It is always the conjunction of a transcendence and an immanence: clearly to recognize what is beyond one is to have received already the means of seeing further into nature. By its apparently specialized and religious character the Christian metaphysics which proceeds from this revitalized reason gives the impression of being a merely regional ontology. But the phrase is quite deceptive, for the ontology of one region has its effects on all the others.

In the course of its pilgrimage reason has to abandon its temporary and rickety resting-places. Such renunciations are seldom pleasant. A metaphysic does not become any easier by becoming supernatural. Furthermore it cannot determine in detail what it owes to the movement of grace and what arises within it under the impulse of nature. Its particular allegiances remain obscure to it; a sacred history and a profane history are inextricably entangled in it; and nature has undergone a sea-change.[2] Again, metaphysics, Christian or non-Christian, must have recourse to various criteria in measuring its approach to the truth; critical philosophy itself finds the principle of non-contradiction too slow and rudimentary a producer of concepts and must add the organizing power of ideas and their conformity with an experience which is both intellectual and moral at the same time. It seems likely, then, that a Christian metaphysics would prove to make use of a number of unprecedented criteria, by which it considers the various aspects successively presented to it as joined together by a spiritual affinity. But all metaphysics, let us repeat, have as their limiting framework the ideas or organisms of ideas which express or symbolize *persons*: and they involve, in addition to theses which are considered as established, hypotheses which are put forward as more or less probable. Grace carries with it a challenge, God's gift requires on our side a certain patience, and a patient mind is the condition of philosophical honesty. The requirements and

[2] It may be added that, if philosophy were always and entirely closed in upon the natural order and did not encounter even implicitly that minimum and incomplete object which suffices to elicit an act of faith, it would be difficult to understand the classical thesis of theology according to which those who follow the light of their reason as best they can and are ready to obey God can attain salvation.

regulations of the reason, and its vocation to develop and to construct, are constant factors, but the directive principles of knowledge and our awareness of them have a plural structure, an uneven and irregular growth and an amphibious status. Reason, considered as a completed system, remains in itself a hope: the bold hope of attaining wisdom.

CONCLUSIONS

1. From St Justin to our time, there have been very various conceptions of Christian philosophy, and the word contains an alarming wealth of possible meanings. The inquiry held by the *Société française de philosophie* in 1931 was the starting-point for a critical examination of the notion which had become altogether necessary. The first result of it was to make clear the distinction between two problems: is Christian philosophy possible?; and, if it is, does it exist as a historical fact?

2. There are four principal interpretations of the notion in question: it may refer to a propaedeutic to Christianity, a philosophy which inherits from revelation, a philosophy which is constituted under the indirect but avowed influence of Christianity, or, finally, a philosophy which, by proclaiming the insufficiency of human nature to resolve the whole problem of man, discerns and in some sense marks out a supernatural gift which would resolve the problem but for which philosophy itself cannot substitute.

3. A historian has a perfect right to speak of a Christian philosophy in a wide sense, or rather of an amalgam of Christian philosophies, to indicate systems which have arisen since the advent of Christianity and are formed in a Christian atmosphere. For example, the metaphysical notion of person has benefited from Trinitarian beliefs, which brought it home to people that a personal life is inconceivable without an interpersonal one, and Christianity encouraged the acceptance of a sort of intersubjective organism unknown to the ancients which gives an altogether fresh depth to the concepts borrowed by the Fathers from Greek philosophy. But the historian, having established these facts, does not normally pronounce upon the nature or the mechanism of the influences

in question. It is enough for him to say that Greek philosophy prepared the way for the formulation of Christianity, and that Christian experience has enriched Greek philosophy. In the end we might find ourselves faced just as easily, if we adopt this point of view, by a monopolization and laicization by philosophy of thought which has naturally germinated, in diffuse form, in a religious civilization, independently of any supernatural reality.

Thus of our four conceptions of Christian philosophy the most strictly accurate seems to be the fourth, that of M. Blondel. It applies, and applies exclusively, to any philosophy which tends of itself to indicate its relationship to a super-nature and to utter an appeal to this supernature, but without thereby becoming confused with the theology of revelation whose imprint it would receive. This recognition on the part of philosophy is the preliminary condition of all conceptual developments which could be considered as philosophical and as Christian at the same time.

4. But these considerations do not exhaust the problem. Everybody seems agreed that the discipline of philosophy belongs strictly to the natural order and that it can have no supernatural mission properly so-called. But M. Blondel's position already suggests to us that the frontiers are not so easy to determine. Furthermore, isn't it a mistake to identify the natural character of an inquiry with its autonomy, as though reflection in becoming Christian ceased to be free and to engage the thinker's personal responsibility? This confusion has vitiated the whole debate. We must at least point out that in the course of history nature can be trans-formed under the influence of grace and that it is both the presupposition of grace and an expression of it.

5. The order of "elevating" grace does not therefore seem to be the true boundary or determining limit of Christian philosophy. Rather the fact is that philosophy examines reality, in any order, only in the perspective of ideas or

organisms of ideas which express personalities. It does not speak of persons by name, and in consequence it is always distinct from a theological meditation or *a fortiori* a spiritual invocation. These principles give us a better understanding of the sort of universality which it can claim.

6. The fact that philosophy is not a matter of personal summons, and that it is always more or less detached from events and from the subject considered simply as such, shows that it cannot substitute for religion. Despite the elements which it has in common with religion, it has its own formally distinct object. For this reason alone, its language and that of Christian faith are not univocal. But since it can partially assimilate a supernatural message in a system of ideas, and since its autonomy is in no way diminished by grace, it is not obliged to fade away in face of Christianity as though its affirmations became erroneous in the presence of the divine Word or had no possible connection with revelation. Its duty is not to efface itself but to enter into this new order by its own free choice: and on this showing an intrinsically Christian metaphysic is possible, despite what so many believers and unbelievers maintain by a sort of tacit agreement which is too easy an escape from the problem for both parties.

7. The conception of reason implied by our conclusions is in line with the traditional doctrine of an analogy between natural knowledge and faith. But it is found in a context which deliberately releases reason from the limits of the strictly natural and demands of it a continual effort of pre-paredness and acceptance, for reason is capable of renewing itself indefinitely in its mission as a universal mediator. The dignity of reason lies in its power to establish contact between all orders and to belong to all of them: its weakness lies in its inability to bring any of them to completion.

Nourished as it is by ingredients of the most diverse kinds, reason is a complex affair. So it need not surprise us that the same word has served to designate both the individual mind and the harmony of all minds and, lastly, the Word which is their pattern and their standard. But in all three cases reason expresses the hidden presence or the summons of an absolute reality. Human or divine, developing or immutable, it makes manifest by its very ambiguity that nothing is isolated in the universe of personal consciousness and that for all terrestrial knowledge there is always something beyond.

SELECT BIBLIOGRAPHY

(An asterisk denotes works by non-Catholics)

*CASSERLEY, J. V. Langmead: *The Christian Philosophy*, London, Faber, 1949.

COLEBURT, R.: *An Introduction to Western Philosophy*, New York, 1957, and London, 1958, Sheed & Ward.

COPLESTON, F., S.J.: *History of Philosophy*, London, Burns & Oates, 1946–60 (6 vols.).

D'ARCY, M. C., S.J., and others: *St Augustine: His Age, Life and Thought*, New York, Meridian Books, 1957, London, Sheed & Ward, 1930.

D'ARCY, M. C., S.J.: *Thomas Aquinas*, London, Benn, 1930.

DE LUBAC, H., S.J.: *The Discovery of God*, London, Darton, Longman & Todd, 1960.

*DODDS, E. R.: *The Greeks and the Irrational*, Berkeley, California Univ. Press and Cambridge, Univ. Press, 1951.

*FARRER, Austin: *Finite and Infinite*, London, Dacre Press, and Naperville, Ill., Allenson, 1943.

FESTUGIÈRE, A. J.: *Personal Religion among the Greeks*, Berkeley, California Univ. Press, 1954.

GILSON, E.: *The Spirit of Mediaeval Philosophy*, London, Sheed & Ward, and New York, Random House, 1955; *Christian Philosophy in the Middle Ages*, London, Sheed & Ward, and New York, Random House, 1955: *Christian Philosophy of St Thomas Aquinas*, New York, Random House, 1956.

HAWKINS, D. J. B.: *Essentials of Theism*, London, 1949, and New York, 1950, Sheed & Ward.

JOLIVET, R.: *Introduction to Kierkegaard*, London, F. Muller, 1950.

LONERGAN, B. J. F., S.J.: *Insight, A Study of Human Understanding*, London and New York, Longmans, 1957.

MARCEL, G.: *The Mystery of Being*, London, Harvill Press, 1950, and Chicago, Regnery, 1951.

MARITAIN, Jacques: *A Preface to Metaphysics*, translated by E. I. Watkin, New York, Sheed & Ward, 1939; *An Essay on Christian Philosophy*, New York, Philosophical Library, 1955; *The Degrees of Knowledge*, London, Bles, and New York, Scribner, 1958.

*MASCALL, E. L.: *He Who Is, a Study in Traditional Theism*, London and New York, Longmans, 1943.

PIEPER, J.: *Happiness and Contemplation*, London, Faber, 1958.

PONTIFEX, Dom Mark: *The Existence of God*, London and New York, Longmans, 1947.

PONTIFEX, Dom Mark, and TRETHOWAN, Dom Illtyd: *The Meaning of Existence*, London and New York, Longmans, 1953.

*REARDON, B. M. G.: *A Christian in Philosophy: Maurice Blondel* (the author points out that there is no exposition of Blondel's thought in English in book form), *Theology*, London, S.P.C.K. and New York, Macmillan, Sept. 1958.

ROUSSELOT, P., S.J.: *The Intellectualism of St Thomas*, London, Sheed & Ward, 1935.

SERTILLANGES, A. D., O.P.: *Foundations of Thomist Philosophy*, London, Sands, and Springfield, Ill., Templegate, n.d.

*TOYNBEE, A. J.: *Greek Historical Thought*, Boston, Beacon Press, 1950.

TRETHOWAN, Dom Illtyd: *An Essay in Christian Philosophy*, London, Longmans, 1954.

The Twentieth Century Encyclopedia of Catholicism

The number of each volume indicates its place in the over-all series and not the order of publication.

All titles are subject to change.